*For Brian Friel.*

First published by The Appletree Press
in 1978 as *Faces of Old Leinster*

Designed by
Spring Graphics Co.

Printed by
The Appletree Press Ltd.

Paper ISBN 0 904651 45 2

Art Ó Broin & Seán McMahon

# Dublin and Leinster

A Photographic and Literary Record 1875-1925

Appletree Press

# Contents

Preface . . . . . . . . . . . . . . . . . . . . . . . . . . . . . . . . . 4
Introduction . . . . . . . . . . . . . . . . . . . . . . . . . . . . . 5
DOWN THE COUNTRY . . . . . . . . . . . . . . . . . . . . 9
AFLOAT . . . . . . . . . . . . . . . . . . . . . . . . . . . . . . 35
THE CITY . . . . . . . . . . . . . . . . . . . . . . . . . . . . . 51
IMPERIAL ECHOES . . . . . . . . . . . . . . . . . . . . . 71
THE TROUBLES . . . . . . . . . . . . . . . . . . . . . . . . 91
AROUND THE PROVINCE . . . . . . . . . . . . . . . . . 99
Index of Authors . . . . . . . . . . . . . . . . . . . . . . . 114
Acknowledgements . . . . . . . . . . . . . . . . . . . . . . 114

# Preface

Our thanks are due to the late Billy English of Athlone; the director and staff of the National Library of Ireland; the staff of the library of the Institute of Continuing Education (NUU), Magee College, Derry, especially Alan Roberts; the staff of the Belfast Central Library; Kevin Etchingham of Dundalk; Cathal O'Shannon; Mike Byrne of Tullamore and the Offaly Research Library; Don Roberts and James Delehanty of Kilkenny; Arnold Crawford of Mountmellick; Séamas de Vál S.P.; John Hayes of Wexford; Harry Fairtlough of Drogheda; Mgr L Ryan of Carlow; Paddy Laird of Dublin; James O'Donnell of Mullingar; and Frank D'Arcy of Derry.

# Introduction

With *Dublin and Leinster* the quartet of Irish faces is complete. The double vision of Ireland on the brink of the modern world has been extended to cover the eastern province. This double vision, originally devised by the compiler of the first volume in the series, Brian Walker, is obtained by the juxtaposition of contemporary pictures and literary excerpts. Such a procedure is both objective and subjective—objective in that the photographs and associated pieces are proper relics of the period, subjective because it is the *surviving* evidence that paints the picture of the past for the present and because the book is made from a personal (and perhaps idiosyncratic) choice of the compilers from these survivals. The result would seem to show that Leinster is a separate part of Ireland, as distinct in its nature and in its appearance as Munster or Connaught or the North.

The most obvious element of distinctiveness of this part of Ireland is, of course, the City—*the great wen*—at once the pride and the despair of the patriot, the invader and the moralist. Because of its separate history, its diverse elements, its place at the centre of land and sea routes, it never seemed to fit the accepted nineteenth-century image of Ireland; and yet for all its complexity and its exoticism it was as Irish

*Bull Alley, Dublin* (Lawrence Collection, National Library).

as the Bog of Allen or the Mountains of Mourne. To say it dominated Leinster is to put it too strongly but politically, morally, culturally and topographically its presence was and is felt. On the great distorted dart-board that a road map presents (a spider's web, if your imagination is darker) all tracks lead to and all forces pull towards the urban centre. At Dundalk, Longford, Carlow or New Ross the power of the magnet is felt.

It is probably fanciful, a kind of self-fulfilling prophecy, but one cannot avoid the impression that by comparison the ancillary counties seem shadowy and their towns however prosperous and their people however busy give the impression of perpetually looking east. The region too, was *English* Ireland. Pale faces were as prevalent as native Irish ones. Gaelic as a spoken language had disappeared, drained from all parts but the wilder north of Co Louth. Fenianism, Land Agitation, 'troubles' played a less dramatic part in Wicklow and Kilkenny, Meath and Carlow than in the west and south; '98 was the last time that Leinster was actively in arms. And yet all ideological movements, whether political, industrial or revolutionary had to have their nerve centres in Dublin. So had the government and the forces of the Crown. If at times travellers got the impression of dehydration or anaemia about these 'home counties' it was not that the people 'down the country' lacked vitality but that the City's needs seemed to drain them.

As for the Dublin Irish they grew up with typical urban suspicion of the rural mind and fear of the empty silences, finding within a few miles of their birthplaces their total universe. Many who sang in pubs and street corners of Killarney's lakes and Bantry Bay were unlikely to have seen either and had no strong wish to; and they viewed with cynical satisfaction and some jealousy the steadily increasing flow of culchies into *their* metropolis. The middle class Catholics and Protestants were beginning to find accomodation each with the other, while the working class obstinately refused to fulfil Engels' prophecies. Matt Talbot was no more untypical of the scene than Jim Larkin. Besides, the City was its own theatre with a ruritanian panoply of public events. The universities, the Castle, the imperial presence, the race meetings, the levees and garden parties provided a rich atmosphere even for the non-participants. The meanest and the grandest almost rubbed shoulders with each other. The finest dwellings cohabited with some of the worst slums in Europe: a short step from the Green brought you to the Cathedral hovels. The Church and State, only officially at odds, dominated the place and when the military presence became too obviously a reminder of a palliated subjection there was always the relief of the civilian police force, the D M P as jolly as a light opera chorus line till the batons came out in 1913.

The writers of Leinster show the same lurch towards the City.

Some of the greatest names in Irish literature are here: O'Casey, Joyce and Synge. Mixed with these are less luminous beings who nevertheless have their own brightness: Padraic Colum, Katherine Tynan, Bram Stoker, Oliver Gogarty, Brinsley MacNamara, James Stephens, Francis Ledwidge. Most were born in Dublin or gravitated towards it in the course of their careers. A matter of little surprise; for, sociological truism or not, the tremors of change begin and end in the centre of greatest population. The literary revival may have been conceived in the remote west but it was born and lived in the city.

The pictures come from several rich archives — French, of Lawrence, Keogh and the careful gleanings of the growing number of local historical and antiquarian societies who have at last succeeded in prodding the people into a sense of the riches of their past. Respect grows with knowledge; impatience turns to sympathy. As we look upon the faces and listen to the voices of these 'faithful departed' we begin to understand ourselves through them, to evaluate more precisely their bequests to us. And we begin to understand that those who do not learn from history are punished by having to experience it themselves.

*Scouts on Killiney Hill*

# Down The Country

SOME features of County Wicklow, such as the position of the principal workhouses and holiday places on either side of the coach road from Arklow to Bray, have made this district a favourite with the vagrants of Ireland. A few of these people have been on the roads for generations; but fairly often they seem to have merely drifted out from the ordinary people of the villages, and do not differ greatly from the class they come from. Their abundance has often been regretted; yet in one sense it is an interesting sign, for wherever the labourer of a country has preserved his vitality, and begets an occasional temperament of distinction, a certain number of vagrants are to be looked for. In the middle classes the gifted son of a family is always the poorest - usually a writer or artist with no sense for speculation - and in a family of peasants, where the average comfort is just over penury, the gifted son sinks also, and is soon a tramp on the roadside.

In this life, however, there are many privileges. The tramp in Ireland is little troubled by the laws, and lives in out-of-door conditions that keep him in good-humour and fine bodily health. This is so apparent, in Wicklow at least, that these men rarely seek for charity on any plea of ill-health, but ask simply, when they beg: 'Would you help a poor fellow along the road?' or, 'Would you give me the price of a night's lodging, for I'm after walking a great way since the sun rose?'

John M Synge *In Wicklow and West Kerry* (Dublin, 1912).

*Wicklow Tramp 1906* (Synge Collection, Trinity College)

SYNGE'S characteristic amalgam of romanticism and wildness is most clearly seen in his attitude to vagrants. The tramp in *The Shadow of the Glen* (1903) is the most complete character, holding some of the quality of Christy Mahon. He loved the travelling-men he met on his many journeys on foot in Wicklow and Kerry and he had almost total empathy with them. He often signed his letters to Molly Allgood 'your old tramp' and he believed that 'in a family of peasants . . .the gifted son sinks . . .and is soon a tramp on the roadside.'

11

*Fair Day Longford c. 1908* (Lawrence Collection, National Library).

## A DROVER

To Meath of the pastures,
From wet hills by the sea,
Through Leitrim and Longford
Go my cattle and me.

I hear in the darkness
Their slipping and breathing.
I name them the bye-ways
They're to pass without heeding.

Then the wet, winding roads,
Brown bogs with black water;
And my thoughts on white ships
And the King o' Spain's daughter.

O! farmer, strong farmer!
You can spend at the fair
But your face you must turn
To your crops and your care.

And soldiers - red soldiers!
You've seen many lands;
But you walk two by two,
And by captain's commands.

O! the smell of the beasts,
The wet wind in the morn;
And the proud and hard earth
Never broken for corn;

I will bring you, my kine,
Where there's grass to the knee;
But you'll think of scant croppings
Harsh with salt of the sea.

Padraic Colum *Wild Earth* (Dublin, 1907).

PADRAIC COLUM (Patrick McCormac Colm) was born in Longford in 1881, the son of the workhouse master of that town. As novelist, playwright and author of many poems he was a considerable figure in the Irish Literary Renaissance. An early Abbey dramatist his naturalistic plays such as *Land* (1905) helped turn the Abbey away from Yeats's earlier vision of its purpose. A friend of Synge and Thomas MacDonagh, the 1916 Proclamation signatory, he died in Enfield, Connecticut in 1972.

IT WAS a cold sunny day early in April; there is a saying that April borrowed twelve days from March, and that is what skins the old cow. On one of these days Marting Macevoy was fencing his barley field, as soon as it got a bit green the cattle would be breaking in over the dry earthen bank. Ever since he came there he had been thinking of planting a right quick set hedge, but like a great many greater and smaller things in the country, it was thought of a long time without being done, put on the long finger as we say. He had gathered a lot of bushes and briars from round the other fields, and that was a good job, too, to get them out of the way of pulling the wool off the sheep. He was laying them along the top of the bank in a thick beard, keeping them in place with stones and scraughs cut off the grass field. It was tedious work and hard on hands and clothes, but he could keep an eye on the servant boy, who was ploughing the next field for turnips. When he looked round he could see, too, though it was near a mile away, the big field at Drummond, and make out his own five acres to a sod, there was a bush at one side and a white stone on the wall at the other. He said to himself:

'For all the harsh wind it's beginnin' to look green, God bless it, but it would take with a dash of rain if it was the will of God. If it turns out well it will pay all, and we'll have a great plenty of straw. My blessin' on him that thought of it, only for him we were broke, horse and fut. Sure we never can ask a day's delay in the rint again or a shillin' abatement. I don't know how I'll ever face Mr. Humphreys. Mary must take the rint to him, 'twas none of her side gave the annoyance. And if it would be hard on me what would it be on that poor angashore of a brother of mine? Mag must go, she has the face of the worl - spake of the divil!''

Here he was struck dumb at the sight of his sister-in-law opening his eyes but it was indeed she coming straight towards him. He turned his back and worked diligently, not seeming to hear her step, but the voice that said, "Good evenin', Marting," was so low and quiet that he had to turn round to see if it was indeed Mag, then he said:

"I wonder, Margaret, to see you here."

"You don't wonder more than I do to see myself, after the way you treated me the last time."

M A Rathkyle, *Farewell to Garrymore* (Dublin, 1912).

M A RATHKYLE' (Miss Marianne Younger) lived in Rathdowney and contributed many stories and sketches to an American magazine called *Ireland*. Her novel, *Farewell to Garrymore* (1917) was reckoned at the time to be among the most realistic books about Irish peasant life. She died in 1917.

*Ploughing at Skerries c. 1903* (Lawrence Collection, National Library).

*The Foys in their motor-car at Church Street, Athlone.* (Phot.
Simmons/Old Athlone Society Coll.).

*Sir Thomas* [*to O'Reilly*]. There's sense in what he says.

*Fogarty.* So, I see it's all a plot, a Yankee plot and swindle. But I'm too wide awake for all of you. And I've backers in the parish priest and all the well-off people. O dear, ay! I could raise a thousand pound to-morrow if I wanted it.

*O'Reilly.* You'll want it, Mr. Fogarty.

*Fogarty.* Oh, yes! So will you to take you out of this. I'm off to rouse the country, me and Mr. Casey. O Lord, ay! You'll smoke me out. You'll cut off sun and wind from me. Ho, ho! It's me will smoke you out and cut off water from you. Wait a bit, my boy! Good day to you, Sir Thomas. Poor old Ned Mulroy! (Goes out.)

*Sir Thomas.* We daren't move an inch if he can raise the money.

*O'Reilly.* You keep your word, Sir Thomas. Press the bank claim on him. Leave the rest to me. Do you think a skunk like that is going to stop my progress?

*Mrs. Walton.* There's fight still left in Stephen J., believe me.

*O'Reilly.* If you stand by me, Mrs. Walton, I defy creation.

*Mrs. Walton.* Oh, I'll stand by you, never fear, my friend.

*Sir Thomas.* But really, Mr. O'Reilly, I don't see my way.

*Patrick.* The country will be on us if we treat him harshly.

*Ned.* In Ireland a man's land is as sacred as his wife. I wonder if I offered Kitty to him now! Kitty and two hundred of a fortune -?

*Mrs. Walton.* The very thing. A suitable match for both of them. [*Pulls Ned aside.*]

*O'Reilly.* My friends, I'm into this. My automobile is starting for a run. If a child or lady [*Bows to Mrs. Walton*] wanders in my way, I'll stop and move them gently. But if a grown-up man plumps down on my track deliberately and plugs his ears, I'll just advance the speed a twist, and rip!! The car may jolt. I'm staring, staring straight ahead. I've got no time to look around for accidents.

*Mrs. Walton.* Stephen J., I hope I'll be allowed a seat in that same car.

*O'Reilly.* The engineer is honoured. [*Bows.*]

*Ned.* The Lord in heaven save us. This man wouldn't stop at anything.

*O'Reilly.* Not if stopping meant destruction to my passengers. [*Takes Sir Thomas aside.*]

*Mrs. Walton* [*aside to Ned*]. You and I, Mulroy, will see about this. You think your daughter is willing?

*Ned.* She'll do it to save her family.

(Curtain.)

William Boyle *The Mineral Workers* (Dublin, 1910).

THE MINERAL WORKERS was the most seriously intended of Boyle's plays but the large cast of characters proved too much for his limited dramatic talent. The story is of a returned American engineer and of his struggles with the conservative small-holders whose lands he hopes to mine. A possible Ibsenesque theme was not developed and Boyle settled for comedy - or indeed, farce - as in his two earlier plays.

*Mrs. Dempsey.* Well, Jerry, what side are you on now?

*Dempsey.* The right side, to be sure, my dear.

*Mrs. Dempsey.* There can't be two of them in the same quarrel. Can there?

*Dempsey.* God help your wits, woman. When a man's in public life there's as many sides as there's people to discuss them with.

*Mrs. Dempsey.* Double-dealing, Jerry. Double-dealing never thrives.

*Dempsey.* There's no more double-dealing in this than selling one man porter and another ginger-beer. You don't argue downstairs with your customers about their tastes in liquor.

*Mrs. Dempsey.* I'm not talking about customers, but about yourself, Jerry.

*Dempsey.* Well, what about me?

*Mrs. Dempsey.* You're like Lanna Macree's dog - a piece of the road with everybody. One minute you're all for Cloghermore and the sky over it, and the next you're all for moderation and the Government. It's the same way with you in everything. You're a publican by trade and a member of the Anti-Treating League for recreation. You denounce

*Blackrock Bazaar Dundalk 1900's* (Lawrence Collection, National Library).

Emigration on the platform, and behind the counter you sell tickets for the shipping companies. You'll go anywhere and subscribe to anything if they'll only let you make a speech about it. [*Dempsey protests by a gesture.*] Jerry, you're a rag on every bush, fluttering to every wind that blows; and [*tenderly*] if you weren't the best husband and the best father that ever broke the bread of life, I'd say you were the biggest rascal in the whole of Ireland.

*Dempsey.* Sure, every one's a rascal in the eyes of somebody.

*Mrs. Dempsey.* And if you don't mind, you'll be a rascal in the eyes of everybody. "Never mix your drinks," my father used to say, and never mix your principles is my advice to you, Jerry.

*Dempsey.* Faith, Catherine, the best of drink is often made by blending.

*Mrs. Dempsey.* Oh, I see!

*Dempsey.* Yes; and the curse of this unfortunate country is that people can't be got to blend their views at all. We all want to run our own spirit into other people raw.

William Boyle *The Eloquent Dempsey* (Dublin, 1909).

WILLIAM BOYLE was born in Dromiskin, Co Louth in 1853. He is best known as the author of three early Abbey plays of small town life: *The Building Fund* (1905) *The Eloquent Dempsey* (1907) and *The Mineral Workers* (1907). They were very popular comedies though Yeats admitted to Synge that he and Lady Gregory found *The Eloquent Dempsey* 'impossibly vulgar'. Boyle withdrew his plays after the Playboy row in 1907. The description of Dempsey, the time-pleasing publican, by his wife, 'You're like Lanna Machree's dog - a bit of the road with everyone' has passed into the language. He died in 1922.

"OCH, IT'S YE that's the play-boy. Shure this very minyet ye have it in yer mind to make the poor lonely widdy, Mrs. Mackesy, on the airliest possible occasion."

"I shouldn't be surprised meself to see her Mrs. Monaghan before long," was Terry's retort.

"That'll do ye now," cried Monaghan, lighting his pipe. "Ye may accuse me o' coortin' whin ye see me scarin' the cattle wid a red tie, an' not before. But go on wid ye there an' if ye don't persuade her before evenin' I'll say ye have no pluck. An' if I wor you to-day, I'd lave the carpentherin' alone an' stick to the joinin'; ye'd find it more profitable."

Monaghan disappeared round Dolan's corner with a laugh, and Terence Mackesy continued his journey down the street. When he arrived at his destination, he paused at the door, and looked up at the signboard. The artist who had inflicted this atrocity on the establishment has passed away, and, as nothing but good may be said about the dead, the design will be here merely reproduced without any accompanying criticism.

dAnIELmaCk
inthErTainminT
for mAn an Baste.

Mrs. Mack had often but in vain, inveighed against the inscription during her husband's life-time, and now that he was a twelvemonth dead, and according to the laws of usage, no longer a moral entity, she thought it high time to replace the monstrosity by something less calculated to drive away respectable customers.

NICHOLAS P MURPHY was at Clongowes Wood College and later was called to the English Bar. His only surviving work is a collection of Midland sketches set in 'Ballybeg', the name of which is taken as in the plays of Brian Friel as the typical Irish small town. He died in 1914.

Nicholas P Murphy *A Corner in Ballybeg* (London, 1902).

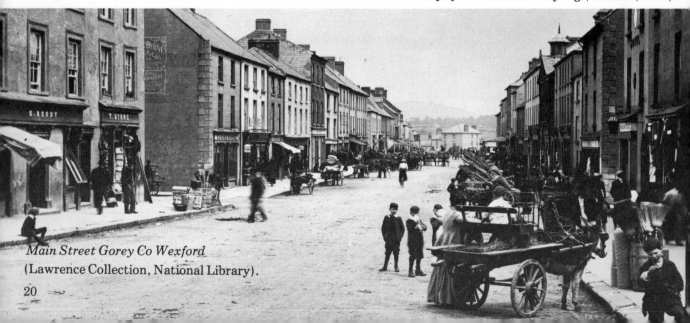

*Main Street Gorey Co Wexford*
(Lawrence Collection, National Library).

*Earl Street, Mullingar* (Lawrence Collection, National Library).

21

*Glenmacnass, Co Wicklow* (Lawrence Collection, National Library).

## THE GLEN OF THE HORSE

"YONDER'S  the cleft in the Mountain, their 'Glen of the Horse,'
Lonely, with bulwarks of granite to left and to right
Lifted above its great boulders, its bracken and gorse
Hiding the rillet that gurgles in giddy delight
Hurrying down to the valley of grey Glenmalure.
What is the legend that haunts it, of wizard or sprite,
Mortal devil or angel or dragon impure?"

"This. I have reason to know it, none living so well.
I am a part of the story that blackens the Glen.
Ever the name of it rings in mine ear like a knell;
Ever its memory darkens my path among men . . .

"It was an evening of summer in red ''Ninety-Eight'
When, as we climbed from the Valley, my troopers and I,
Up by the mule-path, and drew in the breezes, elate,
Reaching the Pass of Imahl and the moorlands on high,
Suddenly rose from a gully the torrents had torn
Wide in the heather a Horseman in Rebel's array,
Leapt with his steed from the cover he lay in forlorn,
Sprang like a hare when it starts at a loud 'hark-away!',
Turned for a moment to scan us, then, striking his spurs
Deep in the sides of his chestnut, away to the height.
Out toward the brown Lugnaquillia through bracken and furze
Rode for his life o'er the moors in the face of the night.

George F S Armstrong *Stories of Wicklow* (London, 1886).

GEORGE FRANCIS ARMSTRONG was born in Co Dublin in 1846 and after graduation from TCD in 1892 he was appointed professor of history and English literature at the then Queen's College, Cork. He was much impressed by his mother's family, the Savages of Ards, published their history in 1888 and added Savage to his name in 1890. He had a high reputation in Ireland towards the end of the century, to the extent that several Irish papers suggested he be appointed Poet Laureate on Tennyson's death in 1892. He died in Co Down in 1906.

*The Abbey, Killeigh* King's
County 1885 (Mathews
Collection). *The Abbey* is a house,
part of which, as the name
suggests was once monastic
property, situated in the village of
Killeigh, five miles south of
Tullamore, King's County. The
property was confiscated during
the reformation and it passed to
the Tarleton family in th late
sixteenth century. The
photograph shows John William
Tarleton (1833-1896) with his
eldest son John. The property was
sold to its present owners, the
Mathews, in 1917.

24

Once upon a time and a very good time it was there was a moocow coming down along the road and this moocow that was coming down along the road met a nicens little boy named baby tuckoo . . .

His father told him that story: his father looked at him through a glass: he had a hairy face.

He was baby tuckoo. The moocow came down the road where Betty Byrne lived: she sold lemon platt.

> *O, the wild rose blossoms*
> *On the little green place.*

He sang that song. That was his song.

> *O, the green wothe botheth.*

When you wet the bed first it is warm and then it gets cold. His mother put on the oilsheet. That had the queer smell.

His mother had a nicer smell than his father. She played on the piano the sailor's hornpipe for him to dance. He danced:

> *Tralala lala,*
> *Tralala tralaladdy,*
> *Tralala lala,*
> *Tralala lala.*

Uncle Charles and Dante clapped. They were older than his father and mother but uncle Charles was older than Dante.

Dante had two brushes in her press. The brush with the maroon velvet back was for Michael Davitt and the brush with the green velvet back was for Parnell. Dante gave him a cachou every time he brought her a piece of tissue paper.

James Joyce *A Portrait of the Artist as a Young Man* (New York, 1916).

JAMES JOYCE (1882-1941) is probably Ireland's greatest modern writer and certainly her most written about. An intense classical and Thomistic training fitted him to be his own best philosophical and aesthetic interpreter and his purpose 'to forge in the smithy of my soul the uncreated conscience of my race' was to his own mind at least, achieved, though whether the triple imposition of silence, exile and cunning was necessary or not has not been proved. *Ulysses* (1922) remains his finest achievement but *A Portrait of the Artist as a Young Man* (1916) is the most revealing. The style of *Dubliners* (1914) a collection of stories about his city, places it as a 19th century work, *Exiles* (1918) his play (rejected by Bernard Shaw for obscenity) is interesting but not great, his poetry is interesting but not great, his poetry is embarrassing and no one has yet been able to prove that *Finnegan's Wake* (1939) was not a joke - Olympian perhaps but a joke all the same.

MORIARTY unwisped the reins from the saddle of the harness and placed them in the small hands of his mistress, who, as an afterthought, had unlatched the Tara brooch and slipped off the cloak.

"Arrah, what have yiz been afther?" said Moriarty, looking back at the strewn garments as though he had only just discovered what the child had been doing. "Glory be to God, if you haven't left the half of yourself behint you on the road - sure what way is that to be behavin'. Now look here, and I'll tell you for onct and for good, if you let another stitch off you, back yiz'll go, dunkey and all, and it's Mrs Driscoll will give you the dhressin' - musha! but you're more thrubble than all me money - *let up wid thim reins and don't be jibbin' the dunkey's mouth!*"

The last sentence was given in a shout as he ran to the donkey's head just in time to avert disaster.

Moriarty sometimes spoke to Miss French as though she were a dog, sometimes as though she were a horse, sometimes as though she were his young mistress. Never disrespectfully. It is only an Irish servant that can talk to a superior like this and in so many ways.

"I'm not jibbing his mouth," replied Miss French. "Think I can't drive! You can hold on to the reins if you like, though, and, see here, you can smoke if you want to."

"It's not you I'd be axin' if I wanted to," replied Moriarty, halting the donkey on a part of the path that was fairly level, so as to get a light for his pipe before they emerged into the sea breeze on the cliff top.

H de Vere Stacpoole *Garryowen* (London, 1910).

HENRY DE VERE STACPOOLE was born in Kingstown in 1863, the son of Rev William Church Stacpoole. He was educated at Malvern College at St Mary's Hospital and practised medicine. His most famous book *The Blue Lagoon* (1915) - a romance of a shipwrecked boy and girl growing up on a South Sea Island - made his reputation. Earlier novels about Ireland were *Patsy* (1908), *Father O'Flynn* (1914). *Garryowen* (1910) is the story of a racehorse.

*Ass and Trap, The Mall, Newtownbarry, Co Wexford. [Lawrence Collection, National Library] c. 1905.*

27

GREG. Is there no chance of raising it locally; there ought to be plenty of money round here.

JOHN. The money is in the banks earning one-and-a-half to two-and-a-half per cent., but it won't come my way. They look on me as mad because I said the engine might be taken up for aircraft work. The fastened on that and made a laugh of me. Aircraft was only one outlet; it means a cheap traction for them here, cheap power for their threshing and ploughing and mowing; the industry would mean more employment for Kilglennon and sweep away the dull, hopeless look of it. Those lads down at the Brothers' Schools—lads who will afterwards be building up the wealth of the States, or Canada, or England, if the prospect of being made Clerk to the Union does not keep them stuck here—these lads would have something to look forward to if their fathers would only back me up now. Think of it, Gregory; think of all those brainy fellows being lost, generation after generation, lost to us for the want of an outlet at home!

GREG. Aye, 'twas only the other day I was trying to track down in my mind where all my school-chums had gone. Only yourself and myself were on the Old Sod.

JOHN. There was Tom Geary, full of divilment. Can you fancy him in a fashionable London practice. And Harry Brown, who used to run that little paper with all the local skits in it, he's managing a big paper in New York. Paddy King is an engineer in India; Callaghan is boss of a contracting firm of builders in South Africa; Lacey is running a huge farm in Canada; Stenson is in the Chinese Customs, top-dog over a crowd of Celestials. What a nation we'd be, Gregory, if all those chaps were back here again, working and prospering as they have done abroad. Lord! Ireland wouldn't be big enough to hold us—nor a nation on the earth strong enough to keep us down.

GREG. John Silent, I'll have to re-christen you. I thought I had some "gift of the gab," but you've developed the most surprising flow of language since I saw you last.

JOHN [smiling]. I don't know when I said as much. I suppose it is getting on my favourite topic, and having you to talk to. Round here they judge you by the paper you read, and a fellow like me, who doesn't read any, is looked on with suspicion. I get sick of the alternate praise and denunciation of Redmond and Carson, Sinn Feiners and Covenanters, William O'Brien and John Dillon. It concerns me more where my socks are made than what was said last night in the Orange Lodge, the Masonic Hall, or the A.O.H.

GREG. "Them's my sentiments," John, and if everyone took the same interest in the origin of their clothes we'd be able to afford much better ones. Look at all the money we spend on the importation of that item alone. Look at all a woman spends; look at all she spends on even one small section—her underwear. Many a man makes a point of getting

THOMAS KING MOYLAN was born in 1885 and became chief clerk of Grangegorman Hospital. He was the author of many stage comedies which became very popular with amateur companies. *The Curse of the Country* deals with the perennial economic problems of emigration and protectionism v. free trade and is notable for the character of the Irish merchant, Darcy Killigan who 'has a shop, a series of them in fact, all under one roof, than which Harrod's Stores never stocked a wider variety of wares. It was his boast that no man, or woman for that matter, needed anything from cradle to coffin that he could not supply.' He died in 1958.

28

"home-grown" collars, ties, and shirts; but ask the average Irishwoman where her underwear is made, and what will she say? [*MOLLIE passes the window and comes to the door.*]

JOHN [*smiling*]. I can guess what she'd say, and I know for certain what the neighbours would say. Catch me asking the average Irishwoman anything about her clothes, or where they came from.

MOLL. [*entering*]. I'm an average Irishwoman, John, but you needn't be afraid to ask anything about my clothes, though from Adam I couldn't tell you where anything I have came from; I'm quite satisfied to get them.

[*JOHN and GREGORY look embarrassed. Then JOHN introduces GREGORY and MOLLIE*].

JOHN. Miss Regan this is Gregory O'Neale, a very old friend of mine. Gregory, Miss Regan. [*They shake hands heartily.*]

MOLL. [*to GREG.*] What wild deeds were you inciting John to do just now?

MALACHY SCALLY came from Kilbeggan, the distillery village where the famous Tullamore Dew was first manufactured. The design of the shop was based on one seen in Liege and it was erected by direct labour with the assistance of the architect T F MacNamara. Scally's business declined afterwards because the shop proved to be too grand for the clients. It is now owned by Glessons.

*Scally's Shop, Williams Street, Tullamore, 1912* (Lawrence Collection, National Library).

## THE DEAD AT CLONMACNOIS.

In a quiet watered land, a land of roses,
   Stands Saint Kieran's city fair:
And the warriors of Erin in their famous generations
   Slumber there.

There beneath the dewy hillside sleep the noblest
   Of the clan of Conn,
Each below his stone with name in branching Ogham
   And the sacred knot thereon.

There they laid to rest the seven Kings of Tara,
   There the sons of Cairbré sleep—
Battle-banners of the gael, that in Kieran's plain of crosses
   Now their final hosting keep.

And in Clonmacnois they laid the men of Teffia,
   And right many a lord of Breagh;
Deep the sod above Clan Creidé and Clan Conaill,
   Kind in hall and fierce in fray.

Many and many a son of Conn, the Hundred-Fighter,
   In the red earth lies at rest;
Many a blue eye of Clan Colman the turf covers,
   Many a swan-white breast.

T W Rolleston
*'The Dead at Clonmacnoise' Sea Spray* (Dublin, 1906).

The Shannon is a glorious river, broad and deep, and brimming over, extending from source to sea a distance of two hundred miles, and 'making its waves a blessing as they flow' to ten Irish counties . . . Six miles from Athlone we pass the Seven Churches of Clonmacnoise (once, as its name signifies, the Eton of Ireland, 'the school of the sons of the nobles') by whom despoiled and desecrated we English need not pause to enquire; and close to these a brace of those famous Round Towers which have so perplexed the archaeological world, and which according to Frank were 'most probably lighthouses which had come ashore at night for a spree and had forgotten the way back again.'

S Reynolds Hole *A Little Tour in Ireland* (London, 1896).

THOMAS WILLIAM HAZEN ROLLESTON was born in Shinrone, King's County in 1857. He was one of John O'Leary's circle of young men though older than Yeats or Hyde. He became an active champion of the Gaelic League in 1896 when Hyde and MacNeill accepted his challenge and were able to prove that Irish could be used as a precise language for philosophy and science. He helped found the Irish Literary Society in England in 1893 and his book *Imagination and Art in Gaelic Literature* (1900) had much influence. He wrote much verse but his lasting claim to literary fame (apart from the lyric printed here) was his editing with Stepford Brook of *The Treasury of Irish Verse* (1900). He died in 1920.

30

*Picnic at Clonmacnoise c. 1902 [Lawrence Collection, National Library]*.

# THE ROADS OF IRELAND

There are many fine roads in Ireland,
  Travelling from the city to the town;
There are straight level roads in Ireland
  And roads for ever going up and down.

There are beautiful fair roads in Ireland,
  Meandering by the woodland and the stream,
Running silver white across the valley
  Out to where the far blue mountains dream.

There are many fine sea roads in Ireland,
  Dashed by the bright salty spray,
Where the warm smell of whin and white clover
  Travel with the traveller all the way.

There are many many roads in Ireland,
Crossing the land from sea to sea.
But of all the highways and the by-ways
  There is only one road for me:

It's the way of high adventure when the morning dew is there,
  It's childhood and the river running free,
It's Youth's delicious rapture and the promises of Life
  When the golden moon has risen from the sea.

There are many many roads in Ireland,
  Long roads, old roads, and new.
Oh! tell me when you're dreaming and romancing,
  Is there only one road for you?

'Hal D'Arcy *Poems* (Dublin, 1930).

Little is discoverable about HAL D'ARCY except that in spite of her name she was a lady. She wrote one novel *A Handful of Days* (1914) and several books of verse including *The O'Donoghue* (1907) and *Poems* (1930).

*Co Wexford Gorey and Courtown Omnibus c. 1912* (Lawrence Collection, National Library).

*The 4½ mile route from Gorey to Courtown which had been serviced by two long cars, was given a bus service in 1912. The service was started by Mrs Boyne of the Railway Hotel who apparently got the vehicle and driver from Scotland. The service ran each of the three summers until the outbreak of war.*

Market days, Dundalk, c. 1905

34

*Arklow Harbour c. 1900 [Lawrence Collection, National Library].*

**Afloat**

*The City of Dublin Steam Packet Company* carried the mail between Kingstown and Holyhead from 1851 to 1920. At first they used paddle-steamships and then from 1896 they used four turbine steamships called after the four provinces of Ireland. They were capable of 24 knots and had a deserved reputation for efficency. In 1920 they were replaced by Railway steamers run by the LNWR.

*Mail Boat, Kingstown c. 1905 [Lawrence Coll., National Library].*

*Th' anám an Dhia* but there it is -
  The dawn on the hills of Ireland!
God's angels lifing the night's black veil
  From the fair, sweet   face of my sireland!
O Ireland isn't it grand you look -
  Like a bride in her rich adornin'?
And with all the pent-up love of my heart
  I bid you the top o' the mornin'!

This one short hour pays lavishly back
  For many a year of mourning;
I'd almost venture another flight,
  There's so much joy in returning -
Watching out for the hallowed shore,
  All other attractions scornin':
O Ireland! don't you hear me shout?
  I bid you the top of the mornin'.

For thirty summers, *asthore machree*,
  Those hills I now feast my eyes on
Ne'er met my vision save when they rose
  Over memory's dim horizon.
E'en so, 't was grand and fair they seemed
  In the landscape spread before me;
But dreams are dreams, and my eyes would ope
  To see Texas' sky still o'er me.

Oh! often upon the Texan plains,
  When the day and the chase were over,
My thoughts would fly o'er the weary wave,
  And around this coast-line hover;
And the prayer would rise that some future day -
  All danger and doubting scornin' -
I'd help to win for my native land
  The light of Young Liberty's mornin'!

*John Locke 'The Exile's Return or Morning on the Irish Coast' in*
Irish Literature V [*Philadelphia, 1904*].

JOHN LOCKE was born in Callan, Co Kilkenny in 1847. He joined the IRB in
1863 and contributed to James Stephens' Fenian journal *The Irish People*.
He had the characteristic career of journalism, prison and exile in America.
His poem, 'The Exile's Return' was almost the anthem of the home-looking
Irish-American. He died in New York in 1889.

WINIFRED LETTS was born in Dublin 1882. She contributed several plays to the early Abbey repertoire, notably *The Challenge* (1909) but her lasting claim to fame is her well-known poem 'A Soft Day' which was printed in the first of two collections of poetry, *Songs of Leinster*.

*New Ross Harbour, Co Wexford, c. 1908 (Lawrence Collection, National Library).*

## THE HARBOUR

think if I lay dying in some land
  Where Ireland is no more than just a name,
My soul would travel back to find that strand
  From whence it came.

'd see the harbour in the evening light,
  The old men staring at some distant ship,
The fishing-boats they fasten left and right
  Beside the slip.

The sea-wrack lying on the wind-swept shore,
  The grey thorn  bushes growing in the sand
Our Wexford coast from Arklow to Cahore -
  My native land.

The little houses climbing up the hill,
  Sea daisies growing in the sandy grass,
The tethered goats that wait large-eyed and still
  To watch you pass.

The women at the well with dripping pails,
  Their men colloguing by the harbour wall,
The coils of rope, the nets, the old brown sails,
  I'd know them all.

And then the Angelus - I'd surely see
  The swaying bell against a golden sky,
So God, Who kept the love of home in me,
  Would let me die.

*Winifred Letts* Songs from Leinster [*London, 1914*].

*Ballyhack Co Wexford [Lawrence Collection, National Library].*

JAMES MURPHY was born in Dublin in 1839 and after some period as a teacher in Bray was appointed Professor of Mathematics to the Catholic University under Newman's successor, Woodlock. He wrote many romantic historical novels about Ireland, most notably *The shan Van Vocht* (1883). He died in Kingstown in 1913.

IT WAS with a heart beating with conflicting emotions that Eugene found himself in the officers' quarters of the Thunderer, wherein at a large table sat the captain and a number of gentlemen resplendent with all the gorgeousness of naval uniform. If he had had the time to analyze these emotions he would have found the principal one to be a vague sense of disappointment and loss and disaster. Not every man in warfare on sea or land must run the risk of these - they are the incidents of his profession; but for others. Simple as was the little barque in appearance that was even then making her rapid way through the deep waters to the bottom, she bore important fortunes. The future of a gallant and brave nation struggling into the light of freedom was in her keeping, and mayhap the safety of a powerful and friendly fleet. He was convinced, from all that he had heard the night before, that the only chance for success attending the great venture France was about to make in Ireland's cause, was in making the Eastern coast their point of debarkation; and that unless the present intention of the Republican leaders were altered, sorrow would come to the cause now engaging the attention of the high-hearted men whom he had left last night - and misfortune to a French army and fleet.

*James Murphy* The Shan Van Vocht [*Extract from* Irish Literature [*Philadelphia, 1904*]].

'Ireland has, practically speaking, no mercantile marine. A few coasting and cross-channel steamers running to continental ports is all that is left of the once great commercial fleet of Ireland ... Why have we not this marine? We have the material in abundance of which sailors are made. We have £50,000 of money lying idle in our banks. It is because we have not the spirit of a free people—because we are taught to be dependent and look to and trust in a foreign parliament when the people of other nations are taught to look and trust in themselves'

*Regatta at Boat Club, Wexford.* [*Séamas de Vál Collection, Oulart, Co Wexford*].

40

IT CHANCED that this Sabbath morning a brigantine was lying alongside the quay, her captain standing near the whell, and a couple of "hands" forward. I had invited them to Trinity Church, and had given some of my little books to them, when, as I was returning to ascend the shore-plank, I saw an old man seated on the windlass forwards. He was dressed unlike an ordinary seaman, wore a tall black hat, black frock-coat, and had the air of a past respectability strongly marked upon his face, which bore the marks of deep care and sorrow. He sat in the hot sunlight, kicking his feet against the deck, and scarcely looked up when I drew near and saluted him.

"I tell you what it is," at last exclaimed he passionately, as I spoke a few words to him, "I have seen sorrow enough to drive any man out of his right senses. I was not always thus," he said, and he looked up with his sunken eyes into my face, "only two years ago I was happy, and look at me now; then I was master of my own ship, now I am before the mast; then I had my dear wife, now I am alone in this earth."

"It comes before me now again," he said dreamily, and his face grew ashen pale, - the snow-crowned hills around - the frozen Neva, - the craft lying frozen up alongside one of those great buildings to which she was secured by iron rings and hawsers. "My men had all left save two, for we were regularly shut up for the winter at St. Petersburg, and these two men after a time got tired of the snow, and ice, and cold, and went home; but the wife, she still stuck to me, and we made the best of it; it was cold and dreary enough, but we loved each other, and were company to one another, though it was so far from home. Well, one of those great men, to whom I had applied, had sent me two Russians as care-takers of the ship, of whom he gave me a good character, and though I never liked their looks much, still I did not like to encourage myself in doubting them; they had little to do with us, nor we with them; they lived forward in the forecastle to themselves, and smoked away, or slept away their time - one man watching by day, another by night. Well, sir, one day," and his voice trembled, "I had to send a particular letter home to the owners, and I did not like to send it by the men, so as I knew the way to the post-office I went myself, and as I returned" - here he grasped the windlass, and trembled violently - "I caught sight of the ship, and there was a dense smoke rising forward and another aft. I rushed down like a madman - you must know it was a very lonely part of the river, and no other ship lay near her - down the companion I ran, calling out, 'Wife, wife! where are you - where?' - oh! that awful moment! I saw her lying dead before me, - her very head cleft in twain with a hatchet blow, and her very ear-rings torn from her ears, and her poor dead face turned downwards. The two Russians had done it, and then set fire to the ship. I don't remember much more then; she was buried; and my heart gave way. I followed her to the grave alone; I heard that the English Consul brought the murderers before the Government, but they did nothing; and now look at me," - and his burning eyes wearily fastened themselves on mine, - "I am broken-hearted, going down from bad to worse, with that awful scene ever rising before my mind. I see it as I sit here; I see it as I take the wheel; I see it as I lay out aloft; I see it in my berth; I see it in my dreams; and he wearily drooped his head upon his chest, and relapsed into silence. "I trust," I said, "that you will see her again, not as when you saw her last, still and pale in death, but radiant in joy, and clothed with the robe of the Redeemer's righteousness."

[Rev] J Duncan Craig, Real Pictures of Clerical Life in Ireland [London, 1875].

THE REV J DUNCAN CRAIG was born in 1831 and after graduation from Trinity took orders. He ministered in Kinsale and Dublin where he was the vicar of Trinity Church in Lr. Gardiner Street. He became an authority on Provencal literature but was in no other sense liberal. His two books, Bruce Reynall MA (1898) and Real Pictures of Clerical Life in Ireland (1875) are noted for their pro-Orange, anti-Catholic bias. Phrases like '—when Rome Rule or Home Rule arrives in Ireland—for the terms are synonymous' appear in his writing but his books give a racy if heavily slanted view of Irish life.

'Every dog has his day.'
  Well, dear, do you remember,
How you and I found a golden day
  In the midst of a bleak December?

You smiled at the chance of our meeting,
  I blushed as I turned away,
While our little world stood by in amaze,
With hands upheld in dismay.

We loosened the chain of our little boat,
  And each took an oar in hand.
You spoke no word, but you looked at me,
  And we rowed for love's sweet land.

You said, 'All earth's beauties I see in your face.'
  I said, 'All earth's music you're speaking.'
And the keel of our little craft grated the while
  On the silvery shore of our seeking.

You looked at me and I smiled on you -
  (O sweet! it was golden weather) -
Then we laughed as the boat glided back from the
                                                                shore
  And we pulled from the land together.

For you thought, perhaps, of another face,
  And I - let pass, you remember,
Not half we said on that summer's day
  We found in a bleak December.

                    Dora Sigerson *Verses* (London, 1893).

DORA SIGERSON SHORTER was born in Dublin in 1866, the eldest daughter of George Sigerson, the Gaelic scholar and scientist. A minor versifier of the Renaissance she was sponsored by George Meredith but came in for rather a lot of criticism for her lack of formal technique. Her most famous poem, 'Sixteen Dead Men' was about the 1916 leaders. 'One Day in December' was written for her husband, Clement Shorter, editor of *The Illustrated London News*. She died in 1917.

42

*Below: Trinity College Regatta, Chapelizod c. 1900* (Lawrence Collection, National Library).

WE are going to talk, if you please, in the ensuing chapters, of what was going on in Chapelizod about a hundred years ago. A hundred years, to be sure, is a good while; but though fashions have changed, some old phrases dropped out, and new ones come in; and snuff and hair-powder, and sacques and solitaires quite passed away - yet men and women were men and women all the same - as elderly fellows, like your humble servant, who have seen and talked with rearward stragglers of that generation - now all and long marched off - can testify, if they will.

In those days Chapelizod was about the gayest and prettiest of the outpost villages in which old Dublin took a complacent pride. The poplars which stood, in military rows, here and there, just showed a glimpse of formality among the orchards and old timber that lined the banks of the river and the valley of the Liffey, with a lively sort of richness. The broad old street looked hospitable and merry, with steep roofs and many coloured hall-doors. The jolly old inn, just beyond the turnpike at the sweep of the road, leading over the buttressed bridge by the mill, was first to welcome the excursionist from Dublin, under the sign of the Phoenix. There, in the grand wainscoted back-parlour, with 'the great and good King William,' in his robe, garter, periwig, and sceptre presiding in the panel over the chimneypiece, and confronting the large projecting window, through which the river, and the daffodils, and the summer foliage looked so bright and quiet, the Aldermen of Skinner's Alley - a club of the 'true blue' dye, as old as the Jacobite wars of the previous century - the corporation of shoemakers, or of tailors, or the freemasons, or the musical clubs, loved to dine at the stately hour of five, and deliver their jokes, sentiments, songs, and wisdom, on a pleasant summer's evening. Alas! the inn is as clean gone as the guests - a dream of the shadow of smoke.

Lately, too, came down the old 'Salmon House' - so called from the blazonry of that noble fish upon its painted sign-board - at the other end of the town, that, with a couple more, wheeled out at right angels from the line of the broad street, and directly confronting the passenger from Dublin, gave to it

something of the character of a square, and just left room for the high road and Martin's Row to slip between its flank and the orchard that overtopped the river wall. Well! it is gone. I blame nobody. I suppose it was quite rotten, and that the rats would soon have thrown up their lease of it; and that it was taken down, in short, chiefly, as one of the players said of Old Drury,' to prevent the inconvenience of its coming down of itself. Still a peevish but harmless old fellow - who hates change, and would wish things to stay as they were just a little, till his own great change comes; who haunts the places where his childhood is passed, and reverences the homeliest relics of by-gone generations - may be allowed to grumble a little at the impertinences of improving proprietors with a taste for accurate parallelograms and pale new brick.

Then there was the village church, with its tower dark and rustling from base to summit, with thick piled, bowering ivy. The royal arms cut in bold relief in the broad stone over the porch - where, pray, is that stone now, the memento of its old viceregal dignity? Where is the elevated pew, where many a lord lieutenant, in point, and gold lace, and thunder-cloud periwig, sate in awful isolation, and listened to orthodox and loyal sermons, and took French rappee; whence too, he stepped forth between the files of the guard of honour of the Royal Irish Artillery from the barrack over the way, in their courtly uniform, white, scarlet, and blue, cocked hats, and cues, and rufles, presenting arms - into his embalzoned coach and six, with hanging footmen, as wonderful as Cinderella's and out-riders outblazing the liveries of the troops, and rolling grandly away in sunshine and dust.

*Sheridan Le Fanu* The House by the Churchyard [*Dublin, 1904*].

SHERIDAN LE FANU was born in Dublin in 1814 the son of a dean of the Church of Ireland and grand-nephew of the dramatist, Richard Brinsley Sheridan. He wrote one historical novel, *Torlogh O'Brien* (1847) but already while still a young man had won a special fame as the author of 'Phadrig Crohore' - an Irish Lochinvar. He is best remembered as the author of such novels as *The House by the Churchyard* (1863) and *Uncle Silas* (1864). His shorter pieces of macabre writing collected in *In a Glass Darkly* (1872) are among the finest and most skilfully wrought examples of the *genre* and in *Carmilla*, easily the finest vampire story ever written, he anticipated his more famous fellow Trinity man, Bram Stoker, who did not produce *Dracula* till 1897. In his time he was editor of *The Dublin University Magazine* and *The Evening Mail*. He died in 1873.

*On the River Liffey at Chapelizod, c. 1904 [Lawrence Collection, National Library].*

CROSSING the bridge we enter Chapelizod once a favourite residence for Dublin citizens, and still possessing some traces of the old world respectability which characterised it at the period of which Le Fanu wrote in his famous novel. Between the two approaches from the main street to the Protestant Parish Church, is an old-fashioned house, which is evidently the actual "House by the Churchyard" that plays so prominent a part in the story.

Weston St J Joyce *The Neighbourhood of Dublin* (Dublin, 1912).

"YOU SEE," were Davie's reassuring words, "there's plenty of room to *sit* upright" (which was strictly true; but I am not very tall, and he is short). "Some people make a point of head-room, but I never mind much about it. That's the centre-board case," he explained, as in stretching my legs out, my knee come into contact with a sharp edge.

I had not seen this devilish obstruction, as it was hidden beneath the table, which indeed rested on it at one end. It appeared to be a long low triangle, running lengthways with the boat and dividing the naturally limited space into two.

"You see she's a flat-bottomed boat, drawing very little water without the plate; that's why there's so little headroom. For deep water you lowere the plate; so, in one way or another, you can go practically anywhere."

I was not nautical enough to draw any very definite conclusions from this, but what I did draw were not promising. The latter sentences were spoken from the forecastle, whither Davies had crept through a low sliding door, like that of a rabbit-hutch, and was already busy with a kettle over a stove which I made out to be a battered and disreputable twin brother of the No. 3 Rippingill.

"It'll be boiling soon," he remarked, " and we'll have some grog."

My eyes were used to the light now, and I took in the rest of my surroundings, which may be very simply described. Two long cushion-covered seats flanked the cabin, bounded at the after end by cupboards, one of which was cut low to form a sort of miniature sideboard, with glasses hung in a rack above it. The deck overhead was very low at each side, but rose shoulder high for a space in the middle, where a "coach-house roof" with a skylight gave additional cabin space. Just outside the door was a fold-up washing-stand. On either wall were long netracks holding a medley of flags, charts, caps, cigar-boxes, hanks of yarn, and such-like. Across the forward bulkhead was a bookshelf crammed to overflowing with volumes of all sizes, many upside down and some coverless. Below this were a pipe-rack, an aneroid, and a clock with a hearty tick. All the woodwork was painted white, and to a less

ROBERT ERSKINE CHILDERS was born in Glendalough Co Wicklow the son of an Irish mother and an English father but was as he often insisted ' . . .by birth, domicile and deliberate choice, an Irishman.' He was educated at Haileybury and Trinity College, Cambridge, but lived in Ireland from 1919. He wrote the famous and prophetic adventure yarn, *The Riddle of the Sands* in 1903 and took a leading part in the Howth Gun-running of 1914. He took the Republican side in the Civil War and was arrested while carrying a gun given to him as a present by Michael Collins. He was court-martialled and shot in Beggars Bush Barracks on 24 November 1922.

jaundiced eye than mine the interior might have had an enticing look of snugness. Some Kodak prints were nailed roughly on the after bulkhead, and just over the doorway was the photograph of a young girl.

"That's my sister," said Davies, who had emerged and saw me looing at it. "Now, let's get the stuff down." He ran up the ladder, and soon my portmanteau blackened the hatchway, and a great straining and squeezing began. "I was afraid it was too big," came down; "I'm sorry, but you'll have to unpack on deck - we may be able to squash it down when it's empty."

*Erskine Childers* The Riddle of the Sands [*London, 1903*].

*Kingstown Harbour 1900 [Lawrence Collection, National Library]*

The Great Eastern docked at Dublin: designed by Brunel and used for laying cables in the Atlantic, this was the first iron-clad vessel of its kind.

*Canal Quay, Bagenalstown, Co Carlow*
(Lawrence Collection, National Library)

The City

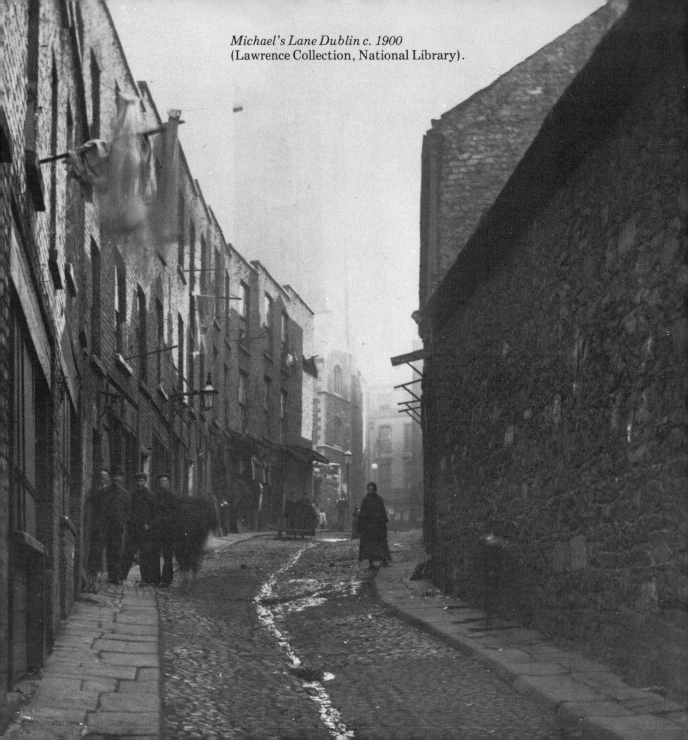

*Michael's Lane Dublin c. 1900*
(Lawrence Collection, National Library).

There's a gray fog over Dublin of the curses,
It blinds my eyes, mavrone; and stops my breath,
And I travel slow that once could run the swiftest,
And I fear ere I meet Mauryeen I'll meet Death.

There's a gray fog over Dublin of the curses,
And a gray fog dogs my footsteps as they go,
And it's long and sore to tread, the road of Connaught.
Is it fault of brogues or feet I fare so slow?

There's a gray fog over Dublin of the curses,
But the Connaught wind will blow it from my way,
And a Connaught girl will kiss it from my memory
If the Death that walks beside me will delay.

(There's a gray fog over Dublin of the curses,
And no wind comes to break its stillness deep:
And a Connaughtman lies on the road to Connaught
And Mauryeen will not kiss him from his sleep - Ululu!)

Nora Hopper, 'The Grey Fog' in *Irish Literature* (Philadelphia, 1904).

FROM 1850 onwards Dublin had increasingly attracted immigrants from the provinces but had never been able to provide enough work for them. So it was that by 1900, 87,000 out of a total population of 300,000 lived in slum tenements and of the 5,000 tenements, 1,500 had been condemned as totally unfit for human habitation. Dublin's infant mortality rate was 168 per 1,000 births while that of the country as a whole was only 101. Tuberculosis and other diseases were rife as was alcoholism.

NORA HOPPER was born in Exeter in 1871, the daughter of an Irish officer in the British Army. Her poetry and prose are very delicate and filled with a rather romantic view of Irish life, as this poem shows. Yeats in his misty period announced that her *Ballads in Prose* (1894) 'haunted me as few books have ever haunted me'. She died in 1906.

"What would it be about, Mick?"

"Well, I'll tell you, Geraghty, what it would be about. It would be an Act for finding out first, by a jury iv reg'lar cliver fellows, in what diraction a lad's taste lay, so that the boy might be taught the right thrade, and not cram him with a thrade that he had no likin' for. Bekase it's the most murdherin' foolishness for a father or mother to say, 'I'll make Tom a carpenther; Jack a sweep; Larry a tinker; and Mat a smith.' The lads is not consulted at all, and they have no likin' or taste for the thrades they are put to, and then what's the consequuince? Why, first it

*Glencree Reformatory c. 1899*
(Lawrence Collection, National Library).

akes twiced as much money and time to make them larn anythin'. econdly, their lugs is well warmed for them, and they're backs well carified bor not gein' quick enough at what they'll never be anythin' at. hirdly, when they're out iv their time and work at their thrades they'll et the blessin' backwards iv everybody that has dailin's with them. 'ourthly, they'll get a revinge against everybody from the abuse they et, and get into no ind iv quarrels and ructions, and to keep up their perrets they take to dhrink. Fifthly, when people come to see the otches they are, they won't imply them, and then the lads commence to tarve and rob to make out a livin', and that's the road to the gallows. Jow, Terry, as I tould you, my Act would remidy that state iv affairs as ar as it could be remidied, bedase the choice ive the thrade wouldn't be eft to the fancy iv parents and guardians, but would be found out by the ury, who would study the child's wishes, and find out what he would be nost inclined for. And a thrade or business a boy has a care for, he will arn it aisy, and if he could do anythin at any thrade he will sartinly do nost at the wan he took a fancy to."

"Well, Mick, I have known boys that if you had a grand jury sittin' on hem, you couldn't find out what was their taste, and you see there you'd e bet."

"No, Terry, my 'Cure for Starvation Act' provides for them sort iv lads, ekase in all the industhrial schools, reformathories, and wherever else hrades was taught, I'd have such boys insthructed in at laist three lifferent thrades, so that if they failed at wan they could turn to another, nd if they failed in all, they could do a little in aich; the same as the big hops does at present, for formerly what is in wan big shop now, was pread over a dozen or more."

"There is somethin' in that, Mick, sartinly, I admit."

"To be sure there is, Terry. You never hear foolishness out iv my mouth t all, bekase, as Lanty often says, 'them that buys him for a fool loses heir money,' so I, for a great dale more raison, say the same ive myself. Jure I'll give an instance in point which comes complate to hand intirely, nd that is in conniction with wan iv my speculations. I'm talkin' now ive he failure iv the Irish Church Missioners to show converts in Jonnaught. You see, Terry, the fathers and mothers iv Missioners didn't know what thrade was shuited to them, and they made them Irish Jhurch Missioners instead iv makin' them tinkers and sweeps, that they vould have taken on to betther, bekase they couldn't be worse as Missioners than they are. But talkin' o' them reminds me that I'd petther now tip the head Missioner a letther, afeerd the former wan went asthray, or the Missioners think it is impossible I could do what I said."

"Yes, Mick, that's a good idea, and you will have plenty iv time, for, ifther Lanty comes in with the thripe, it will take some time to do, before ve can have our dinner."

Mick McQuaid on *Education* in *The Shamrock* Saturday, March 4, 1893,

COL WILLIAM FRANCIS LYNAM though born in Galway in 1845 spent most of his life in Dundrum and Clontarf. After retiring from the 5th Royal Lancashire Militia he lived in almost hermetic solitude. The adventures of his character, Mick McQuaid ran in *The Shamrock* from January 19, 1867 till beyond the author's death in 1894. Mick is the archetypal philosophical witty demotic Irishman whose comical adventures are laced with acute observations upon 19th-century Ireland.

On the beach in front of this dainty mansion a young lady was sitting on a ridge of shingle, bleached by sun and sea-water to perfect cleanliness, which afforded a comfortable resting-place. The young lady seemed much at her ease. Her skirt of blue serge was turned up over a second skirt of white and blue and caught up at the back in what used to be called "fishwife" fashion - the bodice fitting her slight supple figure easily, perfectly; a little foot in a dark-blue stocking, and an incomparable shoe peeped forth as she supported an open book on one knee, and a wide-brimmed sailor hat almost hid her face as she bent over the page.

A big brown boat drawn up beside her made a shelter from the level rays of the sinking sun. Altogether she presented a pretty picture of quiet enjoyment.

As the last strains of the band died away a gentleman in boating attire strolled slowly across the grass, paused, looked round as if searching for somethng, and then came straight over the shingle towards her.

She heard his step and looked at her book with renewed attention, nor did she move till he stood beside her. Then she raised her face, an interesting, rather than a pretty face, somewhat brunette in complexion, and pale, with a warm paleness - a small, oval face, with a delicate chin and a very slight downward curve at the corners of the soft red mouth, that gave a pathetic expression to her countenance when in repose. Her eyes, too, which were her best feature - large eyes, with long, dark lashes, had a wistful, far-away look, more suited to a saint than to their piquante owner.

The man who paused beside her was tall and slender, with a grace of movement not usual in an Englishman. He was darker, too, than ordinary Anglo-Saxons, who rarely possess such blue-black hair and flashing dark eyes as his. His well-cut, refined, but determined mouth was unshaded by moustaches, though a strong growth of black beard showed through his clear olive-brown skin. He smiled a soft, caressing smile as he threw himself on the sand at her feet, saying: "I thought you had gone on the pier with Callander?"

"No; he has gone to the station to meet Mr. Standish, and Mabel has had the honour of a command from the Grand Duchess to drive with her."

The saintly-pathetic expression entirely disappeared, as she spoke with a swift, arch smile, and a

*Esplanade Bray 1903* (Lawrence Collection, National Library).

56

lash of scorn from her "holy eyes."

"Ah," he returned, in an amused tone, "why did *you* not go to meet your beloved guardian?"

"I never meant to go. I came out of the way to listen to the band *here*. Music is so charming as it comes fitfully on the breeze, and I enjoy it most alone."

"Well, it is over now, so I may venture to stay?"

"Oh, yes, if you like! But I am tired of sitting here. I want to match some silks. Do you mind, Mr. Egerton?"

"Not at all. As Madame de Stael says, '*être avec ceux qu'on aime -* '"

"It sounds just as well in English," she interrupted, laughing. "'To be with those we love is all-sufficient, etc., etc., etc.'—yes, it is a pretty sentiment."

"You are not in an amiable mood to-day, Miss Wynn. What book is this? Let me carry it for you. Ah! 'The Great Lone Land.'"

"Yes, it is charming—thank you," giving it to him.

"Don't you think it would be cruel to waste this lovely evening matching silks in a stuffy shop? Let us go along the common towards the pier. We may meet some of your party returning."

"Yes, let us go along by the sea." She turned as she spoke, and directed her steps to a low grassy embankment which protected the common on the shore side.

Annie F Alexander *Blind Fate* (London, 1891).

ANNIE FRENCH ALEXANDER was born in Dublin in 1825, the daughter of Robert French, a Dublin solicitor. She published in all forty novels which ranged from high romance to gothic mysteries. Her best known work was *The Wooing O't* (1875). *Blind Fate* (1891) is a mystery story which led a publisher's hack to contrive the following less than deathless quatrain:

*In Mrs Alexander's tale*
  *Much Art she clearly shows*
*In keeping dark the mystery*
  *Until the story's close.*

She died in 1902.

*Marine Hotel Bray 1903*

(Lawrence Collection, National Library).

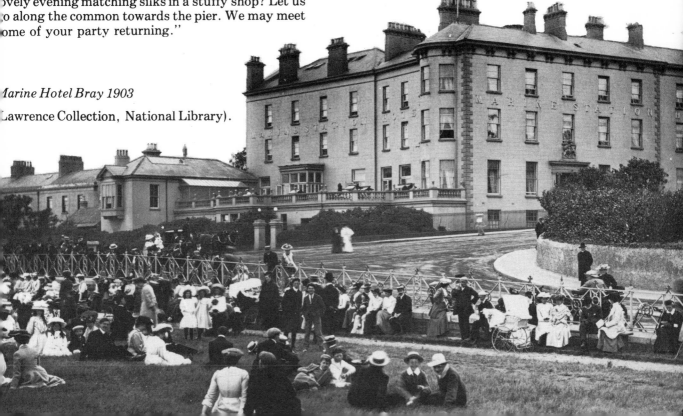

JAMES STEPHENS was born in
Dublin in 1880 (not, as he often used
to claim, on the same day as James
Joyce). He was sent to an industrial
school in 1886 for begging   and
afterwards served as a clerk in
several firms. He soon became
accepted into Dublin's literary circles
as much for his talk as for his writing.
He wrote poems and wildly
imaginative, quirky prose including
*The Crock of Gold* (1912) and *Here
Are Ladies* (1913). He was Registrar
of the National Gallery from 1915 to
1924 and in later life won fame as a
very idiosyncratic broadcaster. He
died in 1940.

58

Her mother knew it was time to get out of bed when she heard a heavy step coming from the next room and going downstairs. A labouring man lived there with his wife and six children. When the door banged she jumped up, dressed quickly, and flew from the room in a panic of haste. Usually then, as there was noting to do, Mary went back to bed for another couple of hours. After this she rose, made the bed and tidied the room, and went out to walk in the streets, or to sit in the St Stephen's Green Park. She knew every bird in the Park, those that had chickens, and those that had had chickens, and those that never had any chickens at all - these latter were usually drakes, and had reason on their side for an abstention which might otherwise have appeared remarkable, but they did not deserve the pity which Mary lavished on their childlessness, nor the extra pieces of bread with which she sought to recompense them. She loved to watch the ducklings swimming after their mothers: they were quite fearless, and would dash to the water's edge where one was standing and pick up nothing with the greatest eagerness and swallow it with delight. The mother duck swam placidly close to her brood, and clucked in a low voice all kinds of warnings and advice and reproof to the little ones. Mary Makebelieve thought it was very clever of the little ducklings to be able to swim so well. She loved them, and when nobody was looking she used to cluck at them like their mother; but she did not often do this, because she did not know duck language really well, and feared that her cluck might mean the wrong things, and that she might be giving these innocents bad advice, and telling them to do something contrary to what their mother had just directed.

The bridge across the lake was a fascinating place. On the sunny side lots of ducks were always standing on thir heads searching for something in the water, so that they looked like only half ducks. On the shady side hundreds of eels were swimming about - they were most wonderful things: some of them were thin like ribbons, and others were round and plump like thick ropes. They never seemed to fight at all, and although the ducklings were so tiny the big eels never touched any of them. Even when they dived right down amongst them. Some of the eels swam along very slowly, looking on this side and on that as if they were out of work or up from the country, and others whizzed by with incredible swiftness. Mary Makebelieve thought that the latter kind had just heard their babies crying; she wondered, when a little fish cried, could its mother see the tears where there was already so much water about, and then she thought that maybe they cried hard lumps of something that was easily visible.

After this she would go around the flowerbeds and look at each; some of them were shaped like stars, and some were quite round, and others again were square. She liked the star-shaped flowerbeds best, and next she liked the round ones, and last of all the square. But she loved all the flowers, and used to make up stories about them.

James Stephens *The Hill of Vision* (London, 1922)

*Winter in St Stephen's Green c. 1904* (Lawrence
Collection, National Library).

Of priests we can offer a charmin' variety,
Far renowned for larnin' and piety;
Still, I'd advance you, widout impropriety,
Father O'Flynn as the flower of them all.

*Here's a health to you, Father O'Flynn,*
*Slainté, and slainté, and slainté agin;*
  *Powerfullest preacher, and*
  *Tinderest teacher, and*
*Kindliest creature in ould Donegal.*

Don't talk of your Provost and Fellows of Trinity,
Famous for ever at Greek and Latinity,
Dad and the divels and all at Divinity,
  Father O'Flynn'd make hares of them all.
  Come, I venture to give you my word,
  Never the likes of his logic was heard,
    Down from Mythology
    Into Thayology,
  Troth! and Conchology, if he'd the call.

Och! Father O'Flynn, you've the wonderful way wid you,
All the ould sinners are wishful to pray wid you,
All the young childer are wild for to pray wid you,
  You've such a way wid you, Father avick!
  Still, for all you're so gentle a soul,
  Gad, you've your flock in the grandest conthroul;
    Checkin' the crazy ones,
    Coaxin' onaisy ones,
  Liftin' the lazy ones on wid the stick.

And though quite avoidin' all foolish frivolity,
Still at all seasons of innocent jollity,
Where was the play-boy could claim an equality
  At comicality, Father, wid you?
  Once the Bishop looked grave at your jest,
  Till this remark set him off wid the rest:
    "Is it lave gaiety
    All to the laity?
  Cannot the clargy be Irishmen too?"

*Here's a health to you, Father O'Flynn,*
*Slainté, and slainté, and slainté agin;*
  *Powerfullest preacher, and*
  *Tinderest teacher, and*
*Kindliest creature in ould Donegal.*
  Alfred P Graves *Father O'Flynn and other Irish Lyrics* (London, 1899).

ALFRED PERCIVAL GRAVES was born in Dublin in 1846, the son of Charles Graves who afterwards became Bishop of Limerick. He graduated from Trinity in 1871 and became in turn assistant editor of *Punch*, Home Office Clerk and Inspector of Schools. He was the father by his second wife of Robert Graves the romantic poet and gadfly critic, whose book of World War I, *Goodbye to All That* (1929) spurred him to write a most entertaining book of reminiscences called *To Return to All That* (1932). Famous as the author of the song 'Father O'Flynn' and as a translator from Irish his greatest contribution to the Gaelic Revival was in the sphere of Irish music. He died in 1940.

60

As part of the Tercentenary celebrations on Thursday, 7 July 1892 a
procession was held from the Examination Hall to the Leinster Hall where
delegates from other universities presented addresses. Later in the day there
was a garden party at The Royal Hospital, Kilmainham and in the evening a
performance of Sheridan's *The Rivals* (an appropriate choice for an assembly
of Irish dons) was given at the Gaiety Theatre. The celebrations were
presided over by Provost George Salmon, then a distinguished
septuagenarian. At the Tercentenary banquet, the evening before, Lecky the
distinguished historian had prayed ' . . . that the spirit that animated this
university in the past may still continue. Whatever fate may be in store for us,
whatever new powers may arise, may this university at least, be true to
itself . . .'

*Trinity College, Dublin Tercentenary 1892*
(Larry O'Connor Collection, Dublin).

*Fisherwomen in front of old Tholsel, Wexford, 1895*

## HERSELF AND MYSELF
An Old Man's Song.

'T was beyond at Macreddin, at Owen Doyle's weddin',
  The boys got the pair of us out for a reel.
Says I: "Boys, excuse us." Says they: "Don't refuse us."
  "I'll play nice and aisy," says Larry O'Neil.
So off we went trippin' it, up an' down steppin' it -
  Herself and Myself on the back of the doore;
Till Molly - God bless her! - fell into the dresser,
  An' I tumbled over a child on the floore.

Says Herself to Myself: "We're as good as the best of them."
  Says Myself to Herself: "Sure, we're betther than gold."
Says Herself to Myself: "We're as young as the rest o' them."
  Says Myself to Herself: "Troth, we'll never grow old."

As down the lane goin', I felt my heart growin'
  As young as it was forty-five years ago.
'T was here in this *bóreen* I first kissed by *stóireen* -
  A sweet little colleen with skin like the snow.
I looked at my woman - a song she was hummin'
  As old as the hills, so I gave her a *pogue*;
'T was like our old courtin', half sarious, half sportin',
  When Molly was young, an' when hoops were in vogue.

When she'd say to Myself; "You can court with the best o' them."
  When I'd say to Herself: "Sure, I'm betther than gold."
When she'd say to Myself: "You're as wild as the rest o' them."
  And I'd say to Herself: "Troth, I'm time enough old.'

*Patrick Joseph McCall, 'Herself and Myself' in* Irish Literature VI (Philadelphia, 1904),

PATRICK JOSEPH MCCALL was born in Dublin in 1861. His *Fenian Nights Entertainments* was serialised in *The Shamrock*. These were tales of the Fianna told in 'seanchaí' style and very popular in their day. He is chiefly remembered as the author of many fireside songs including 'Follow Me Up To Carlow', 'Kelly of Killaine' and 'Boolavogue'. He died in 1919.

TALL, and gaunt, and stately, was "Master Ben;" with a thin sprinkling of white, mingled with the slightly-curling brown hair, that shaded a forehead, high, and somewhat narrow. With all my partiality for this very respectable personage, I must confess that his physiognomy was neither handsome nor interesting: yet there was a calm and gentle expression in his pale grey eyes, that told of much kind-heartedness - even to the meanest of God's creatures. His steps were strides; his voice shrill, like a boatswain's whistle; and his learning - prodigious! - the unrivalled dominie of the country, for five miles round was Master Ben.

Although the cabin of Master Ben was built of the blue shingle, so common along the eastern coast of Ireland, and was perched, like the nest of a pewit, on one of the highest crags in the neighbourhood of Bannow; although the aforesaid Master Ben, or (as he was called by the gentry) "Mister Benjamin," had worn a long black coat for a period of fourteen years - in summer, as an open surtout, which flapped heavily in the gay sea-breeze - and in winter, firmly secured, by a large wooden pin, round his throat - the dominie was a person of much consideration, and more loved than feared, even by the little urchins who often felt the effects of his "system of education." Do not, therefore, for a moment, imagine that his was one of the paltry hedge-schools, where all the brats contribute their "sod o' turf," or "their small trifle o' prateens," to the schoolmaster's fire or board. No such thing; - though I confess that "Mister Benjamin" would, occasionally, accept "a hand of pork," a kreel, or even a kish of turf, or three or four hundred of "white eyes," or "London ladies," if they were presented, in a proper manner, by the parents of his favourite pupils.

In summer, indeed, he would, occasionally, lead his pupils into the open air, permitting the biggest of them to bring his chair of state; and while the fresh ocean breeze played around them, he would teach them all he knew - and that was not a little; but, usually, he considered his lessons more effectual, when they were learned under his roof; and it was, in truth, a pleasing sight to view his cottage assemblage, on a fresh summer morning; - such rosy, laughing, romping things! "The juniors," with their

*Artane Schools* (Lawrence Collection, National Library).

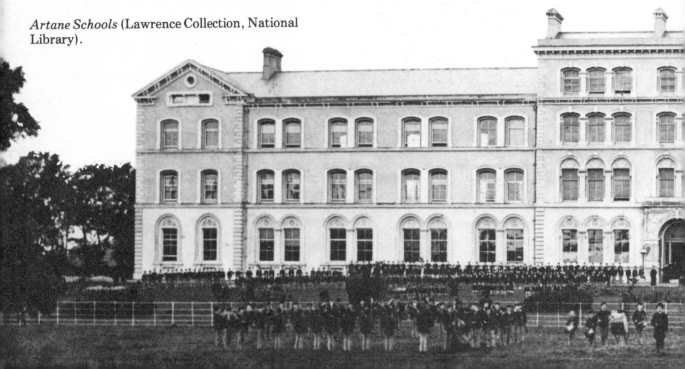

rich curly heads, red cheeks, and bright, dancing eyes, seated in tolerably straight lines - many on narrow strips of blackened deal - the remnants, probably, of some shipwrecked vessel - supported at either end by fragments of grey rock; others on portions of the rock itself, that "Master Ben" used to say, "though not very asy to sit upon for the gossoons, were clane, and not much trouble." "The Seniors," fine, clever-looking fellows, intent on their sums or copies - either standing at, or leaning on, the blotted "desks," that extended along two sides of the school-room, kitchen, or whatever you may please to call so purely Irish an apartment: the chimney admitted a large portion of storm or sunshine, as might chance; but the low wooden partition, which divided this useful room from the sleeping part of the cabin, at once told that Master Ben's dwelling was of a superior order.

Mrs S C Hall *Sketches of Irish Life and Character* (London, 1909).

MRS C HALL (nee Anna Maria Fleming) was born in Dublin in 1800 but spent much of her long life in England. She had a prodigious output of verse, novels, burlettas and opera. Her most appealing books are those which deal with Ireland and which are based upon girlhood memories of life in Wexford and upon frequent visits. Her observations as a visitor to Ireland are a rich source for the detail of Irish life in the 19th-century. She seems to have remained professionally Irish in spite of her exile. She died in 1887.

Founded by Edmund Rice of Callan, Co Kilkenny at the beginning of the 19th-century, the Christian Brothers established schools in most towns of any size. The schools gave a religiously committed education to the children of lower and lower-middle class Catholics. The Christian Brothers remained apart from the national school system with its mild attempt at religiously integrated education. Later in the century the Christian Brothers were noted for their skill in preparing pupils for the new state examinations. In the early 20th century, for one reason or another, a large proportion of the revolutionaries passed through the Christian Brothers schools. To the Brothers the revolution was the proof of their contention that they had taught the children of the Irish poor and had taught them well.

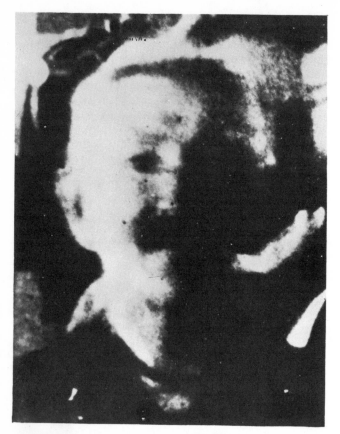

*Matt Talbot [Taken from a group Phot. of workers of the firm of T. & C. Martin] c. 1915* (Paddy Laird Collection).

MATT TALBOT was born in 1856 in the poor area of Dublin's north side. He lived for most of his long life in Rutland Street where he looked after his mother until she died. He was employed as a storeman in T & C Martin's timberyard on the North Wall. In the lockout of 1913, in spite of O'Casey's accusation, he supported the workers' stand but refused to have anything to do with violent picketing. In his young days he was a heavy drinker and a close friend of the original of O'Casey's character, 'Fluther' Good, in *The Plough and the Stars* (1926). Later on he led a life of asceticism and prayer. He died at the age of 69 in Granby Lane, on his way to the Dominican Church in Dominick Street.

[*The silhouette of the tall figure again moves into the frame of the window speaking to the people.*]

PETER [*unaware, in his enthusiasm, of the speaker's appearance, to FLUTHER*]. I was burnin' to dhraw me sword, an' wave it over me -

FLUTHER [*overwhelming PETER*]. Will you stop your blatherin' for a minute, man, an' let us hear what he's sayin'!

VOICE OF THE MAN. Comrade soldiers of the Irish Volunteers and of the Citizen Army, we rejoice in this terrible war. The old heart of the earth needed to be warmed with the red wine of the battlefields . . Such august homage was never offered to God as this: the homage of millions of lives given gladly for love of country. And we must be ready to pour out the same red wine in the same glorious sacrifice, for without shedding of blood there is no redemption!

[*The figure moves out of sight and hearing.*]

FLUTHER [*gulping down the drink that remains in his glass, and rushing out*]. Come on, man; this is too grand to be missed!

[*PETER finishes his drink less rapidly, and as he is going out wiping his mouth with the back of his hand he runs into the COVEY coming in. He immediately erects his body like a young cock, and with his chin thrust forward, and a look of venomous dignity on his face, he marches out.*]

THE COVEY [*at counter*]. Give us a glass o' malt, for God's sake, till I stimulate meself from th' shock o' seein' th' sight that's afther goin' out!

ROSIE [*all business, coming over to the counter, and standing near the COVEY*]. Another one for me, Tommy; [*to the BARMAN*] th' young gentleman's ordherin' it in th' corner of his eye.

[*The BARMAN brings the drink for the COVEY, and leaves it on the counter. ROSIE whips it up.*]

BARMAN. Ay, houl' on there, houl' on there, Rosie!

ROSIE [*to the BARMAN*]. What are you houldin' on out o' you for? Didn't you hear th' young gentleman say that he couldn't refuse anything to a nice little bird. [*to the COVEY*] Isn't that right, Jiggs? [*The COVEY says nothing.*] Didn't I know,

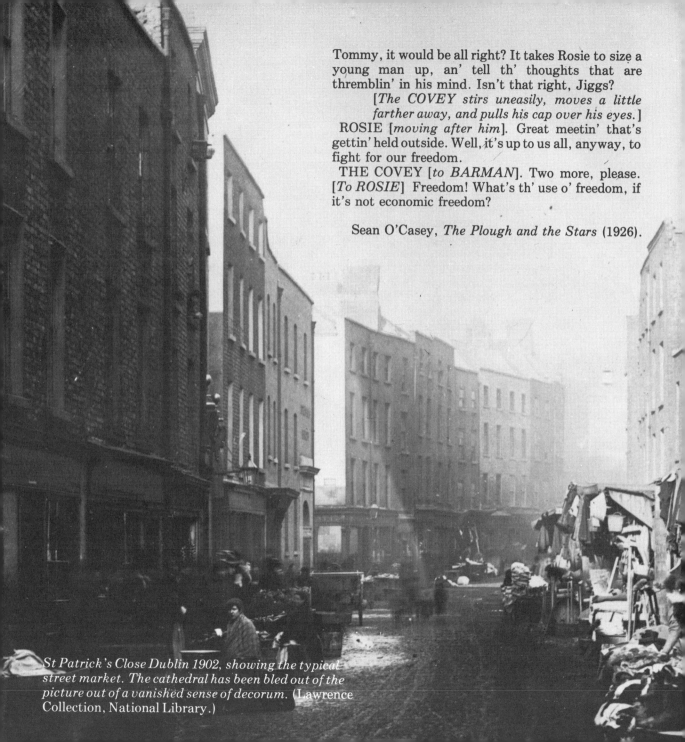

Tommy, it would be all right? It takes Rosie to size a young man up, an' tell th' thoughts that are thremblin' in his mind. Isn't that right, Jiggs?

[*The COVEY stirs uneasily, moves a little farther away, and pulls his cap over his eyes.*]

ROSIE [*moving after him*]. Great meetin' that's gettin' held outside. Well, it's up to us all, anyway, to fight for our freedom.

THE COVEY [*to BARMAN*]. Two more, please. [*To ROSIE*] Freedom! What's th' use o' freedom, if it's not economic freedom?

Sean O'Casey, *The Plough and the Stars* (1926).

*St Patrick's Close Dublin 1902, showing the typical street market. The cathedral has been bled out of the picture out of a vanished sense of decorum.* (Lawrence Collection, National Library.)

*Rathmines Road, Dublin, c. 1900.*

Royal visit 1903, Grafton Street, Dublin

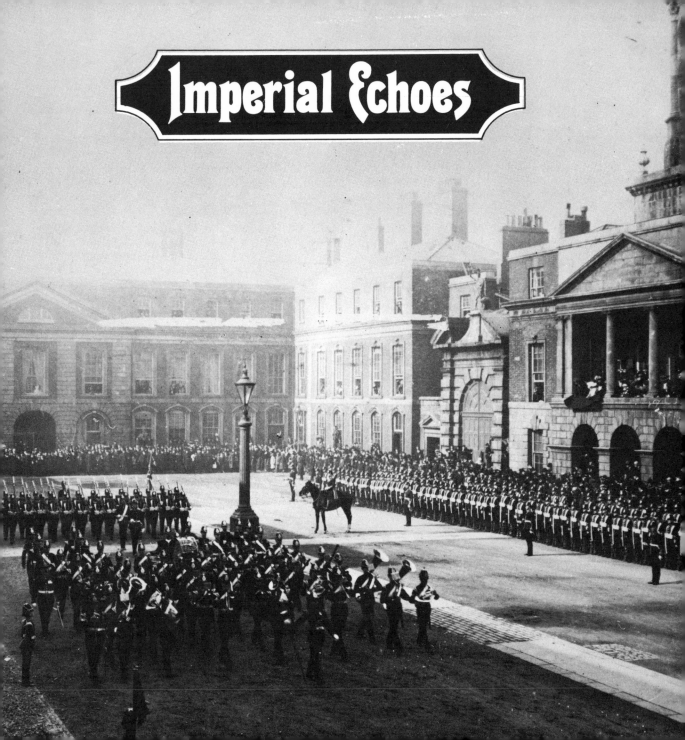

THE annual occasion had come round once more, and, duty over for the day, the afternoon of March 17th saw Sergeant O'Callaghan, in all the glory of best tunic, with buttons highly polished, boots properly shone, trousers nicely stretched, sallying from the barracks, "every inch a soldier," to find the house of Mr. Kelly, whither he had been invited to spend the afternoon and evening in the company of a few friends.

Kelly was a retired sergeant of the 200th, who had left the Service on the expiration of his time, and now lived on his "pinsion," supplemented by "a bit av civilian wurrk." He was a lone widower, whose house was kept by his daughter, and had been O'Callaghan's faithful friend for many years.

There are traits about a smart soldier's walk which seem magnetic to one's vision. The upright carriage, the easy, regular stride, the free and graceful head-poise, the steady, fearless glance. And such was Pat O'Callaghan's on this glorious afternoon, well exemplifying the admonition of an old drill instructor to a squad of recruits, "Never mind if yer pockets contain only the price of a pint, walk as if you owned the side of the street you are on, and were shortly coming in for the other side."

"Ah, Pat, me bhoy, sure an' I've bin afther thinkin' av ye the whole blissid day! How are ye, at all, at all? Permit me to introjuce ye to

*Curragh Camp Co Kildare* (Lawrence Collection, National Library).

ex-Sergeant Maloney, late av the Cowldstrame Guarrds, an' two or three av me civilian friends."

Such was the reception accorded to O'Callaghan on his arrival at Kelly's house.

The introduction over, a bottle of whisky appeared, the cards were produced, and the first part of the visit was spent in quiet enjoyment. Later on came supper, more whisky, anecdotes, music and songs, and by midnight the revellers were in a somewhat hilarious condition.

"Come, Maloney, ye great hulkin' blaygard, jist tell the comp'ny in yer best shtoile yer wan an' only shtory, how ye visited Her Majesty the Queen (God bless her!) an' how she thrated ye to a dhrop av the crathur."

At this Maloney, a big, raw-boned, grizzled Irishman, with a humorous twinkle in his blue eyes, awakes from semi-repose, and, pulling himself together, favours the company with the following yarn.

Frank Byrne *An Irish Stew*
(London, 1916).

FRANK BYRNE is known to literary history as the author of a series of sketches of Irish life called *An Irish Stew*. His phonetic rendering of the brogue becomes at times extreme but the picture of Ireland he gives in his six stories is realistic and not unsympathetic.

Her inches were hardly proportionate to her years, and these measured three. She balanced the deficiency by breadth, and toddled about on the fattest of short legs. She was not pretty after the angelic pattern, and was all the more engaging.

It would be difficult for her biographer to say which were the more adorable; her smile, that raced like a pink radiance from the soft little chin to the crystal blue eyes, or the two perpendicular lines of thought and fearful anxiety that sometimes sprang between the mobile brows, and generally furnished the occasion for stamping her foot at some refractory subject, or were brought into play by an earnest insistence on having the unanswerable answered without delay.

As most of her hours were spent out-of-doors, and hats were antipathetic to her, it followed that few of her subjects enjoyed sight of the carefully combed and curled little poll that left her mother's hands every morning. Instead, they had the more disturbing, if less elegant, picture of fine brown silk rolling and shaking, like the floss of a King Charles, in the dearest confusion imaginable round and about the bright little face. The invasion of curls just permitted the pretty upward play of brown eyelashes against the protruding arch of brow, so that the big blue eyes looked out from a forest of winter shade. She had the divinest of mouths, an arched rosy bud, formed as a child's mouth rarely is, sweet and perfectly shaped, with an imperious claim upon kisses. Not to wish to kiss her, was to prove yourself inhuman. She was never dirty, though not exactly a precisian in the matter of raiment. It would not be safe to trust her with an orange, if it were intended she should sit upon the chairs of civilization, an emblem of spotless childhood; but she could be relied upon any day to pass a neighbourhood where mud-pies were being manufactured and not succumb to the burning temptation to bemire herself.

Such was Norry, the uncrowned queen of a remote little town on the edge of a glorious Irish lake. Like the Oriental philanthropist, she loved her fellow-men. Her existence was based on the first law of Christianity, with such a surprising result that her fellows of all classes, creeds, sexes, and ages worshipped her.

She was not of the order of female infant that is content to stay indoors and play with dolls. Nor were outdoor games the chief delight of her life. What she liked was the making and sustaining of universal acquaintances.

She woke with the dawn preoccupied with the fortunes of Tommy This and Molly That, and chattered about them while she graciously submitted to the encroachments of soap, water, bath-towel, and brush; and she was still discoursing of them in passionate interludes while Marcella fed her upon bread and milk and porridge in the kitchen.

She it was who welcomed all new-comers into the town—tramps, travellers, and visitors. Her formula was as rigid and unchanging as royal etiquette. She drew no line between beggars and noblemen, but simply said to the trousered male: "Man, what's your name?" If there were any geniality in the reply (and there usually was), she as invariably added: "The

blessings of Dod on you. Kiss me!" Upon her lips, however, the command took the form of *tish*. The person in petticoats she addressed as "'oman," and if the 'oman happened to be accompanied by a baby, it was an exciting moment for Norry.

Hannah Lynch *Autobiography of a Child* (London, 1899).

HANNAH LYNCH was born in Dublin in 1862 and was the most literary of the young ladies who joined Anna Parnell's *Ladies Land League* in 1880. When Parnell's paper, *United Ireland*, was suppressed and its editor, William O'Brien, was sent to jail she removed the type to Paris and edited it there. Her most famous book of fiction, *Autobiography of a Child* (1899) caused something of a stir because of the unabashed detail of the reminiscence and the excellence of the writing. Much travelled and the author of many books describing her journeys she died in 1904.

The system of police however in Ireland presents some defects. It is too military in its organisation, and not sufficiently civil or domestic. The barrack mode of life makes the men indolent. It does not appear customary for them to parade the towns and country in beats, as in England. On fair and market days the constables are seen here and there among the people, and on the occasion of a party or faction fight, or in the case of an arrest or a search for arms, they muster in force, but otherwise they are very idle.'

An Englishman *A Walking Tour Round Ireland in 1865* (London, 1867).

*Girl on Horse Tricycle/RIC Depot/Phoenix Park c. 1899* (Lawrence Collection, National Library).

The Gallant Irish yeoman
　　Home from the war has come,
Each victory gained o'er foeman,
　　Why should our bards be dumb?

How shall we sing their praises
　　Or glory in their deeds,
Renowned their worth amazes,
　　Empire their prowess needs.

So to Old Ireland's hearts and homes
　　We welcome now our own brave boys
In cot and hall; 'neath lordly domes
　　Love's heroes share once more our joys.

Love is the Lord of all just now,
　　Be he the husband, lover, son,
Each dauntless soul recalls the vow
　　By which not fame, but love was won.

United now in fond embrace
　　Salute with joy each well-loved face.
Yeoman, in women's hearts you hold the place.

Oliver St J Gogarty *'Ode of Welcome'* (Dublin, 1902).

OLIVER ST JOHN GOGARTY, born 1878, was the great Corinthian of his period. Renowned for his poetry, drama, athleticism, wit and style he was a skilful surgeon, an aviator, the man who owned Ireland's first Rolls-Royce (a butter coloured one) and a senator of the Irish Free State. Joyce's description of him as 'stately plump Buck Mulligan' is somewhat inaccurate as far as the 'plump' is concerned but stately he was and Buck he became to the great pleasure of Dublin. His poetry and novels are in eclipse but his wit and Graecian temper is disclosed in *As I Was Going Down Sackville Street* (1937) and *It Isn't This Time Of Year At All* (1954) which are still celebrated. The piece published here was an *Ode of*

*Welcome* printed in *Irish Society* in June 1902 to celebrate the return of the Irish regiments after their victorious campaigns in the Boer War. It should be read acrostically for Gogarty's alternative message. He died in 1957.

*Marlborough Barracks c. 1900* (Lawrence Collection, National Library).

"Read out the names!" and Burke sat back,
  And Kelly drooped his head.
While Shea - they call him Scholar Jack -
  Went down the list of the dead.
Officers, seamen, gunners, marines,
  The crews of the gig and yawl,
The bearded  man and the lad in his teens,
  Carpenters, coal passers - all.
Then, knocking the ashes from out of his pipe,
  Said Burke in an offhand way:
"We're all in that dead man's list, by Cripe!
  Kelly and Burke and Shea."
"Well, here's to the Maine, and I'm sorry for Spain,"
  Said Kelly and Burke and Shea.

"Oh, the fighting races don't die out,
  If they seldom die in bed,
For love is first in their hearts, no doubt,"
  Said Burke; then Kelly said:
"When Michael, the Irish Archangel, stands,
  The angel with the sword,
And the battle-dead from a hundred lands
  Are ranged in one big horde,
OUr line, that for Gabriel's trumpet waits,
  Will stretch three deep that day,
From Jehoshaphat to the Golden Gates -
  Kelly and Burke and Shea."
"Well, here's thank God for the race and the sod!"
  Said Kelly and Burke and Shea.

Joseph Clarke, 'The Fighting Race' in *Irish Literature II* (Philadelphia, 1904).

JOSEPH IGNATIUS CONSTANTINE CLARKE was born in Kingstown in 1846. He joined the Board of Trade in 1863 and remained there till 1868 when he resigned 'for patriotic motives'. Afterwards he had a distinguished career as journalist and editor in America. He wrote one of the many 19th-century plays about Robert Emmet in 1888 and a 'metrical romance', *Malmorda* in 1893, beginning
  To me by early morn
  Came memories of old Ireland by the sea.
'The Fighting Race' about the Spanish-American War of 1898 is the only one of his poems to have lasted. He died in 1925.

MULLINGAR BARRACKS was built in 1814-1815 and hardly surprisingly named after the Irish-born hero of Waterloo. Wellington Barracks it remained until 1922 when Irish troops under Brig McGuire took over on January 10. For the rest of the year it was the demobilisation centre for the stood-down RIC. The barracks was closed in 1928 and not reopened till 1939 at the beginning of the Emergency. Both photographs are taken from the main gate, the squad facing the camera from the Manchester Regiment and the others from the Connaught Rangers who garrisoned the place in 1904.

*Military Barracks, Mullingar 1904* (Lawrence Collection, National Library).

*Somer's Fort c. 1897* (Lawrence Collection, National Library).

"All but one, remember that—all but one!" said the priest.

"Thank ye kindly, Father, I shan't forget. Thank ye, Andy, an' you, too, young sir; I'm much beholden to ye. I hope some day I may have it to do a good turn for ye in return. Thank ye kindly again, and good-night." He shook my hand warmly, and was going to the door, when old Dan said:

"An' as for that black-jawed ruffian, Murdock—" He paused, for the door suddenly opened, and a harsh voice said:

"Murtagh Murdock is here to answer for himself!" It was my man at the window.

There was a sort of paralyzed silence in the room, through which came the whisper of one of the old women:

"Musha! talk iv the divil!"

Joyce's face grew very white; one hand instinctively grasped his riding-switch, the other hung uselessly by his side. Murdock spoke:

"I kem here expectin' to meet Phelim Joyce. I thought I'd save him the throuble of comin' wid the money."

Joyce said in a husky voice:

"What do ye mane? I have the money right enough here. I'm sorry I'm a bit late, but I had a bad accident bruk me arrum, an' was nigh dhrownded in the Curragh Lake. But I was goin' up to ye at once, bad as I am, to pay ye yer money, Murdock." The Gombeen Man interrupted him:

"But it isn't to me ye'd have to come, me good man. Sure, it's the sheriff himself that was waitin' for ye', an' whin ye didn't come" - here Joyce winced; the speaker smiled - "he done his work."

"What wurrk, acushla?" asked one of the women. Murdock answered, slowly:

"He sould the lease iv the farrum known as the Shleenanaher in open sale, in accordance wid the terrums of his notice, duly posted, and wid warnin' given to the houldher iv the lease."

There was a long pause. Joyce was the first to speak:

"Ye're jokin', Murdock. For God's sake, say ye're jokin'! Ye tould me yerself that I might have time to git the money. An' ye tould me that the puttin' me farrum up for sale was only a matther iv

forrum to let me pay ye back in me own way. Nay, more, ye asked me not to tell any iv the neighbors, for fear some iv them might want to buy some iv me land. An' it's niver so, that whin ye got me aff to Galway to rise the money, ye went on wid the sale, behind me back - wid not a soul by to spake for me or mine - an' sould up all I have! No, Murtagh Murdock, ye're a hard man, I know, but ye wouldn't do that! Ye wouldn't do that!"

Murdock made no direct reply to him but said, seemingly to the company generally:

"I ixpected to see Phelim Joyce at the sale to-day, but as I had some business in which he was consarned, I Kem here where I knew there'd be neighbors - an', sure, so there is."

He took out his pocket-book and wrote names: "Father Pether Ryan, Daniel Moriarty, Bartholomey Moynahan, Andhrew McGlown, Mrs. Katty Kelligan - that's enough! I want ye all to see what I done. There's nothin' undherhand about me! Phelim Joyce, I give ye formil notice that yer land was sould an' bought be me, for ye broke yer word to repay me the money lint ye before the time fixed. Here's the sheriff's assignment, an' I tell ye before all these witnesses that I'll proceed with ejectment on title at wanst."

Bram Stoker, *The Snake's Pass* (London, 1891).

BRAM STOKER in Dublin in 1847 was called afer his father, Abraham Stoker, a Dublin Castle clerk. Though bookish and solitary as a child he became a successful athlete at Trinity and there developed the interest in theatre that drew him from the safety of the Civil Service and led him to the more colourful and certainly more dramatic office of manager to Henry Irving. His first published work was *The Duties of Clerks of Petty Sessions in Ireland* but the fame of this was eclipsed by a gothic romance called *Dracula* (1897). Few of many books written during a lifetime of prodigious labour are still of interest the only one to come near the success of *Dracula* being *The Lair of the White Worm*. His only work set in Ireland was *The Snakes Pass* (1891) from which this excerpt so reminiscent of his friendly rival, Le Fanu, was taken. He died of exhaustion in 1913.

*Soldiers and families on Killiney Strand c. 1904*
(Lawrence Collection, National Library).

This is the Children's War, because
  The victory's to the young and clean.
Up to the Dragon's ravening jaws
  Run dear Eighteen and Seventeen.

Fresh from the Chrisom waters pure,
  Dear boys, so eager to attain
To the bright visions that allure,
  The fierce ordeal, the red pain.

The light is yet upon their curls:
  The dream is still within their eyes;
Their cheeks are silken as a girl's,
  The little Knights of Paradise.

O men with many scars and stains,
  Stand back, abase yourselves and pray!
For now to Nineteen are the gains
  And golden Twenty wins the day.

Brown heads with curls all rippled over,
  Young bodies slender as a flame,
They leap to darkness like a lover;
  To Twenty-One is fall'n the game.

It is the Boy's War. Praise be given
  To Percivale and Galahad
Who have won earth and taken Heaven.
  By violence! *Weep not, but be glad.*

KATHERINE TYNAN was born in Clondalkin in 1861. An active Parnellite she left after the O'Shea affair. She became a member of the O'Leary salon where she met Hyde and formed a passionate but demure friendship with the young Yeats. She wrote many books of poems and light novels. Her poetry has a freshness and an innocence that is characteristic of a woman who for all her fame and company retained the simple catholicism of her girlhood. One of her last appearances in print was in a letter to the *Irish Times* of April 21, 1928. She died in 1931.

Katherine Tynan 'The Children's War' from *Late Songs* (London, 1917).

## THE MERRY POLICEMAN

I was appointed guardian by
The Power that frowns along the sky,
To watch the tree and see that none
Plucked of the fruit that grew thereon.

There was a robber in the tree,
Who climbed as high as ever he
Was able, at the top he knew
The apple of all apples grew.

The night was dark the branch was thin,
In every wind he heard the din
Of angels calling - "Guardian, see
That no one climbs upon the tree."

And when he saw me standing there
He shook with terror and despair,
But I said to him - "Be at rest,
The best to him who wants the best."

So I was sacked, but I have got
A job in hell to keep me hot.

The Dublin Metropolitan Police were (like the City of London Police in the metropolitan area) a force distinct from the general constabulary, the RIC. The force dates from 1836. By 1901 their district included 36 square miles manned by six divisions of uniformed men and seventh division (G Division) of detectives, known as 'G-men' long before Hoover, and the main non-military adversaries of Michael Collins. Their height regulations (at least six feet) made them in general a taller force than the RIC and they took great pride in their dignified appearance which was added to by their tall silver-faced helmets. They were unarmed and bitterly opposed a suggestion made in 1917 that they be amalgamated with the RIC. They pointed out with pride that they were a city and civil force unlike the RIC which was rural and semi-military. The time of their greatest unpopularity was during the lock-out of 1913. Their best known member is the folk-hero constable with the polysyllabic name, 'Mor-i-ar-i-tee.'

*Dublin Castle Guard* (Lawrence Collection, National Library)

CLAVERING sat on the side of an extremely narrow bed and looked at the horn lantern which hung from a bracket in the wall. There was so little room that by stretching out his arms he could span the cell from side to side; but, as this fact had the one merit of ensuring him privacy - since the guard and the prisoner and the prisoner's bed could not all fit in together - he minded it the less.

Straight opposite him, sunk deep in the old masonry of the Bermingham Tower, was an unglazed slit about a foot square.

In the three days since his arrest he had not been able to glean much of the fate of his fellow-conspirators, beyond the negative fact that he was so far the only one in government hands - the sole harvest of Rathlin's carefully-prepared reaping.

They had extracted nothing from him by question or cross-question, by cajolery or threat; but neither had they told him anything. He felt like a live man snatched suddenly into a tomb, with the knowledge that he had left those he valued most in the world in imminent peril.

Miriam Alexander *The Port of Dreams* (New York, 1913).

MIRIAM ALEXANDER was born in Birkenhead but was educated in and later lived in Dublin. A strong supporter of the Gaelic League she left it about the same time as Hyde for much the same reasons. Her best novel, *The Port of Dreams* (1912) is set in Ireland and Scotland at the time of the '45 and contains a dramatic account of Prince Charlie's escape. The novel has the 'modern' theme of cowardice.

At the Vice-regal lodge, the Chief Secretary meets the officials and the 'crows'. Next day he goes to the Castle, curious perhaps to see that notorious institution of which he has heard so much. As he approaches the place he beholds or may behold a conspicuous building hard by, from which a green flag flies defiantly. 'What the devil is that?' he may ask; for in his general ignorance he may take the building to be part of the castle. However he soon finds himself close to the castle gates and is perhaps consoled by seeing the Union Jack fluttering in the breeze. 'But,' he asks, 'what is this building which flies the emblem of Irish nationality at the very gates of the citadel?' He is told that it is the City Hall. If he is a typical Chief Secretary he says, 'Damned rebels' and takes shelter in the fortress.

R Barry O'Brien *Dublin Castle and the Irish People* (London, 1912).

Within the great hall of the Castle of Kilkenny had assembled, in two days after the arrest of Beatrice, the court of the county Palatine, at which she should be tried for the murder of her husband. This spacious apartment was crowded by the feudal lords of the territory governed by de la Spenser, and its passages and approaches were guarded by their retainers. In the principal seat, which was placed upon the dais, sat the Lord Eustace le Poer, according to his seignorial dignity as Seneschal of the district. The chair of state in which he reclined was canopied with richly embroidered tapestry, on which was emblazoned the royal arms of England and the achievements of the houses of le Spenser and le Poer. The Seneschal was attired in the costume of a civilian, his long and flowing robes giving increased dignity to his somewhat mournful aspect; his eye intelligent and was guarded in front and at the closely fashioned sleeves and cuffs with rich fur, and girded by an embroidered girdle buckled about the waist. Over this tunic he wore a mantile of gorgeous velvet, arranged with considerable elegance, and drawn over his right shoulder and across the left arm. The countenance of the feudal lord had assumed an expression of deep sorrow, which none doubted that he truly felt; but, as befitted his office and high jurisdiction, it was calm and dignified. Beneath the Seneschal sat Walter Cotterill, of Kells, sergeant-at-law, who was to speak to the accusation. This functionary was of a grave and somewheat mournful aspect; his eye intelligent and contemplative, his lip inquisitorial, and his hair of an iron grey. No one would hope favour from him, or fear injustice. He was habited in his long full-slieved gown. From his girdle depended his official badge of distinction, the ink horn, with its accompanying pen-case. His head was uncovered, but on his left shoulder rested, attached to the neck of his gown, a circular cap composed of a roll of velvet of rich material. From this hung a long broad band or scarf which was gathered into his girdle; to the other side of this cap a loose hood was attached which fell negligently about his head and shoulders. At his girdle he wore the gypciere or large purse common at the period. Around the hall and seated within canopied niches, or stalls, formed of dark oak, and which had, above each, the banner of arms belonging to the feudal baron to whom it appertained, were assembled the lords of the county Palatine all arrayed in their massive mail suits, the iron sternness of their array being somewhat softened by the graceful draperies of their richly embroidered surcoats. Beneath those leaders upon a bench reserved for them sat the sovereign of the corporation and some of the most wealthy burgesses of Kilkenny. Before the superior judge was placed the prisoner, and at her right hand sat Thomas Derkyn, the lieutenant of de Cantaville, beside whom stood a young and elegant-looking knight, who was known to be Robert Cantaville, the nephew and successor of the murdered chieftain. The unfortunate lady, Beatrice de Cantaville, reclined in the chair placed for her, evidently very much exhausted.

Paris Anderson *The Warden of the Marshes* (Kilkenny, 1884).

PARIS ANDERSON was a lieutenant in the Kilkenny Militia and is known to have lived in Dublin in 1837. His only novel, *The Warden of the Marshes* was published in 1884. It is set in fourteenth-century Kilkenny and has as one of its characters the famous witch, Dame Alice, 'the love-lorn Lady Kyteler' of Yeats's poem 'The Tower'. The book's main interest is in the historical accuracy of the description of the dress etc. of the period.

*Visit of the duke and duchess of York to the marquis and marchioness of Ormond, 1899.*
*Front L—R: Lady Eva Dugdale, Viscountess de Vesci, Marchioness of Ormonde, Duchess of York, Lady Beatrice Butler, Lady Constance Butler, Hon. Hugh Downey.*
*Back L—R: Viscount de Vesci, W T Seigne, Sir Charles Cust, Duke of York, Marquis of Ormonde, Lord F Fitzgerarld, Mr Monerliffe, Earl of Eva.*

EDWARD VII AND ALEXANDRA arrived in Dublin on 21 July 1903, their visit previously arranged for March 1902 having been cancelled owing to poor relations between Dublin and London at that time. The visit coincided with the safe passage through the Lords of the Irish Land Purchase Bill and this was regarded, perhaps a little desperately as a good omen. The Dublin Corporation refused by 40 votes to 37 to offer an address of welcome and William M Murphy had the wit to refuse a knighthood. The visit was the usual sequence of visits to schools, hospitals and the like accompanied by appropriate overeating. Mannix, the president of Maynooth at the time avoided an awkward situation by flying the King's racing colours instead of the Union Jack. The Royal party left from Cork on August 1, full of the 'warmest regard' for the Irish people.

*Kilkenny High Street, decorated for the visit* *Edward VII and Queen Alexandra, (Lawren* Collection, National Library).

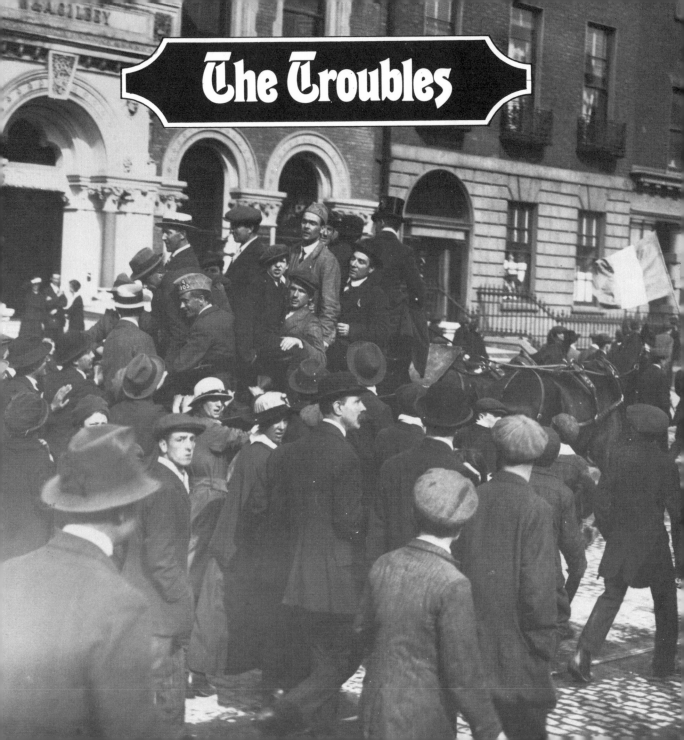

# The Troubles

THE IRISH WORKER was founded by Jim Larkin in 1910 as the organ of his Irish Transport and General Workers Union. It became the workers' main newsheet during the labour troubles of 1913. These began with the dismissal of members of the tramway workers who were Transport Union members and was followed by a general lock-out of 24,000 Dublin men and women. Larkin and Connolly had joined forces and in face of extreme police and army brutality the Irish Citizen Army was formed on 23 November 1913. (Sean O'Casey's first published book was a history of the Army of which he was a member. It was published in 1914 by Maunsel at 1d.) The workers' headquarters were at Liberty Hall, the offices of the ITGWU in Beresford Place. The lock-out ended in apparent failure in January 1914 but its effects were widespread both socially and politically. The head lines in the photgraph refer to the failure of a government commission to bring the two sides together in December 1913. The Daily Herald was for many years the leading English Labour paper.

Of the events in SEAN O'CASEY's early life few made such an impression upon him as the labour agitation of 1912-1913 which led to the formation of the Citizen Army. Jim Larkin became his hero and his strident play *The Star Turns Red* (1940) was dedicated 'to the men and women who fought through the Great Lockout of 1913'. In *Juno and the Paycock* (1924) his most popular play it was characteristic that the role of women in labour agitation should be appreciated and emphasised.

*Mary* [*tying a ribbon fillet-wise around her head*]. I don't like this ribbon, ma; I think I'll wear the green - it looks betther than the blue.

*Mrs. Boyle.* Ah, wear whatever ribbon you like, girl, only don't be botherin' me. I don't know what a girl on strike wants to be wearin' a ribbon round her head for, or silk stockins on her legs either; it's wearin' them things that make the employers think they're givin' yous too much money.

*Mary.* The hour is past now when we'll ask the employers' permission to wear what we like.

*Mrs. Boyle.* I don't know why you wanted to walk out for Jennie Claffey; up to this you never had a good word to say for her.

*Mary.* What's the use of belongin' to a Trades Union if you won't stand up for your principles? Why did they sack her? It was a clear case of victimization. We couldn't let her walk the streets, could we?

*Mrs. Boyle.* No, of course yous couldn't - yous wanted to keep her company. Wan victim wasn't enough. When the employers sacrifice wan victim, the Trades Unions go wan betther be sacrificin' a hundred.

*Mary.* It doesn't matther what you say, ma - a principle's a principle.

*Mrs. Boyle.* Yis; an' when I go into oul' Murphy's tomorrow, an' he gets to know that, instead o' payin' all, I'm goin' to borry more, what'll he say when I tell him a principle's a principle? What'll we do if he refuses to give us any more on tick?

*Mary.* He daren't refuse—if he does, can't you tell him he's paid?

*Mrs. Boyle.* It's lookin' as if he was paid, whether he refuses or no.

Sean O'Casey, *Juno and the Paycock* (London, 1925)

*Workers on the steps of Liberty Hall, 1913* (Keogh
Collection, National Library).

## THE PRICE OF FREEDOM

MAN of Ireland, heir of sorrow,
  Wronged, insulted, scorned, oppressed,
Wilt thou never see that morrow
  When thy weary heart may rest?
Lift thine eyes, thou outraged creature;
  Nay look up, for man thou art,
Man in form, and frame, and feature,
  Why not act man's god-like part?

Think, reflect, inquire, examine,
  Is it for this God gave you birth -
With the spectre look of famine,
  Thus to creep along the earth?
Does this world contain no treasures
  Fit for thee, as man, to wear? -
Does this life abound in pleasures,
  And thou askest not to share?

Look! the nations are awaking,
  Every chain that bound them burst!
At the crystal fountains slaking
  With parched lips their fever thirst!
Ignorance the demon, fleeing,
  Leaves unlocked the fount they sip;
Wilt thou not, thou wretched being,
  Stoop and cool thy burning lip?

History's lessons, if thou'lt read 'em,
  All proclaim this truth to thee:
Knowledge is the price of freedom,
  Know thyself, and thou art free!
Know, O man! thy proud vocation,
  Stand erect, with calm, clear brow -
Happy! happy were our nation,
  If thou hadst that knowledge now!

Denis F McCarthy, *Poems* (Dublin, 1884).

Colonel Maurice Moore, the younger brother of the writer, George Moore, was born at Moore Hall, the family home in Co Mayo. He became a colonel in the Connaught Rangers and as a military expert and a close personal friend of Redmond was an obvious choice to become Inspector-General of the Irish Volunteers when that force was founded by Eoin MacNeill on 25 november 1913.

Eleven months before the Ulster Volunteers had been formed to defend the position of Ulster within the Union. MacNeill had analysed this and other moves in the North in an article published in *An Claidheamh Soluis*, the Gaelic League newspaper. This was later issued as a pamphlet, 'The North Began' and the conclusions reached by MacNeill encouraged the IRB, the radical wing of nationalism, to form a similar body themselves. When the meeting at the Rotunda, Dublin, established the force, it was in fact under the control of the IRB, although many Redmondites were members. The movement spread rapidly over the country, as had MacNeill's earlier movement, The Gaelic League. In the case of Athlone, the subject of our picture, it incorporated an earlier Midland Volunteer Force which had been established two months before.

DENIS FLORENCE MCCARTHY was born in Dublin in 1817 and followed a not untypical 19th-century career as a better-off Irish Catholic. He studied law was called to the bar but did not practise, dabbled in journalism, wrote verse, translated Calderon and became Newman Professor of English Literature. In an unsigned review in the *Catholic University Gazette* 1854, the writer, almost certainly Newman, himself, said of his poetry that, 'beautiful as they are and undoubtedly popular, promise ever more than they display.' His earliest poems were written for the newly-founded *Nation* and his main publications are *The Bell Founder* (1857), *Book of Irish Ballads* (1869) and *Poems* (1884). He died in 1882.

*Volunteer parade being reviewed by Colonel Maurice Moore, December 1914 in Athlone (Phot. Simmons, Old Athlone Society).*

The Kilkenny by-election of August 1917 was the last of a series of four that year in which the Sinn Fein member ousted the sitting Redmondite. The others were at North Roscommon, South Longford and East Clare (where de Valera had his momentous victory in July). As a result of the aftermath of 1916 majority opinion had gone over to the more radical nationalism. This change was confirmed when the older nationalist party was routed in the general election of 1918.

*Markiewicz addressing Sinn Fein supporters at Co Kilkenny election 1917* (Keogh Collection, National Library).

MARTIN:       I know who it was
Hung the blue flowers over the decent cross,
Who put the white flowers into the earth itself,
Who bought the cross maybe, and who, I'll swear,
Made the perpetual masses go up
From the slow priests like a thin incense drifting
Before the throne of God.
MICHAEL.       Though it's all finished
I'll tell you Martin, I would give big money
Put into your fist now, God help me so,
To have that knowledge, so I would.
MARTIN.       I'll tell you.
Have you ever searched out in your sleeping
By a slow hand comes from the hills?
MICHAEL.       I have not;
Not lately; when I was a boy.
MARTIN.       Ah, surely,
Are not those the shining hours men do be having?
I was one time waked that way: something came
And drifted about me, falling from the sky,
Or rising from the earth. Then I went up
Through the grey darkness creeping from the room,
And looked out to a world that the big years
Cannot destroy. Over the Seven Churches
The wood was scarfed in a white drifting mist
In the world's greyness; and, just like a spirit

Thinking and thinking in a kind of coat
That the wind blew about, it sat there dreaming,
While from the middle of itself a song
Came bursting out. It was all quiet that time;
There was nothing about so early as that;
But just that kind of spirit there whose heart
Went bursting up and breaking into a song
Where all songs mixed, that filled up all the world,
And went up in a tumult to the sky.
And I, Michael, I could have been burned up
With the gladness came on me; I could not move,
  trembled so that time.

Darrell Figgis, *Teigue* (Dublin, 1918).

*O'Connell Street, April 1916* (Keogh Collection, National Library).

DARRELL FIGGIS (alias Michael Ireland) was born in Rathmines in 1882. He was taken to India as a child but returned to Ireland in 1913. His was the main influence (according to himself) in the Howth gun-running of 1915. Prominent as a Free State back-room boy, he drew up the constitution for the new state. He committed suicide after an unhappy love-affair in 1925. He published a book of poetry, *A Hill of Vision*, in 1909 and a novel, *Children of the Earth* (1918). *Teigue*, an unactable, sub-Yeatsian verse-play was written in 1918.

The destruction of Sackville Street was partly brought about by looters but most of the damage was done by the ruthless use which the British made of artillery. Connolly was mistaken in his belief that a capitalist power would not destroy property. The efficient use of field guns was one of the reasons the insurgents were so quickly defeated. By the Friday of Easter Week the flames engulfing the street had reached the GPO and Pearse and garrison had to leave by Henry Street. They surrendered next day. Perhaps £2m. worth of damage had been done to the street.

Immediately after the insurrection of 1916 about 3,500 people were arrested. Of these nearly 2,000 were sent to England for internment but after further enquiries 1,300 were released and most of the others were held only until Christmas. Of the leaders fifteen were executed and 75 given penal servitude for various terms. It was these who were released in the summer of 1917, their zeal for independence hardened by their stay in enemy prisons.

PADRAIC PEARSE was born in Dublin in 1879 the son of an Irish mother and an English father. He was educated at the Christian Brothers School in Westland Row and graduated from the Royal University, became a barrister but rarely practised. His keen interest in the Irish language led to reasonable attempts at writing in that language and effective work for its restoration as editor of its journal, *An Claidheamh Soluis*. His ideal of a free and Gaelic Ireland led to the founding of St Enda's, a school for boys at Rathfarnham. He joined the IRB in America and became first President of the Provisional Irish Republic which was promulgated on the steps of the GPO on Easter Monday, 1916. He and his brother Willie were executed in Kilmainham on May 3rd, 1916.

## FORNOCHT DO CHONAC

Fornocht do chonac thú,
A áille na háille,
'S do dhallas mo shúil,
Ar eagla go stánfainn.

Do chualas do cheol,
A bhinne na binne,
'S do dhúnas mo chluas,
Ar eagla go gcloisfinn.

Do bhlaiseas do bhéal,
A mhilse na milse,
Is do chruas mo chroí,
Ar eagla mo mhillte.

Do dhallas mo shúil,
Is mo chulas do dhúnas,
Do chruas mo chroí,
Is mo mhian do mhúchas.

Do thugas mo chúl
Ar an aisling do chumas,
'S ar an ród do romham
M'aghaidh do thugas.

*The burial of Arthur Griffiths, 1920* (Lawrence Collection, National Library).

# Around The Province

## THE DEATH OF DIOGENES,
## THE DOCTOR'S DOG.


### VETERINARY SURGEON
                    Take muzzle from mouth,
And the can from his tail;
He's as dead from the drought
As the deadly doornail.
I fear he has found hydrophobia - not even Pasteur
    may avail.

### DOCTOR
When I rambled around
  In the ground that was Greece,
I was given the hound
  By the King's little niece;
And rather were finded ere I found him to gaze on his
    saddest surcease.

### CHORUS [*Scholars of the House*]
He was given the hound
  By the seed of a King,
For the wisdom profound
  Of his wide wandering.
But was it the donor, or owner, or dog that was led by
    a string?


*The poem was written for the Dublin University
Magazine [14 February 1903] and should be spoken
with a 'w' for 'r' lisp.*

*John Pentland Mahaffy* (Keogh Collection, National
Library) *1917.*

SIR JOHN PENTLAND MAHAFFEY was born in 1839 in
Vevey, Switzerland, the son of a Donegal clergyman
who was Chaplain to the British Embassy in Geneva. He
entered Trinity in 1855 and took orders and was elected
Fellow in 1864. He was given the chair of Ancient History
in 1871 and became Provost after much delay and
despair in 1915, a post he held until his death in 1919. He
was a polymath noted for the breadth rather than the
precision of scholarship. Famous for his rather bullying
wit he was responsible for such epigrams as 'Irish bulls
are always pregnant'. He is also remembered as the man
who refused to join the platform party at the Thomas
Davis Centenary celebrations (20 November 1914)
because of the presence of 'that man Pearse'. He apoteo
Gogarty in much the same way as earlier he had
befriended Wilde and had considerable influence upon
his writings.

WADEBRIDGE [*putting down the book*]. It is not for me to stand between her crime and its punishment.

THE BISHOP [*gratified*]. Ah!

WADEBRIDGE: Nor for me to stand between her and you.

THE BISHOP [*mystified*]. And me?

WADEBRIDGE. The woman condemned to death in your name, as you say, was Mabel Debenham.

THE BISHOP [*in a strangled voice*]. Mabel Debenham! . . . killed her child . . . What child?

WADEBRIDGE. As I believe, your child.

THE BISHOP [*almost screaming*]. My child!

WADEBRIDGE [*producing an envelope*]. Judge for yourself. There is the photograph of mother and child taken a month ago.

THE BISHOP [*glaring at it*]. Mabel and . . . taken a month ago . . . my child, and she had the heart to kill !

WADEBRIDGE. As you had the heart to kill her.

THE BISHOP. To . . . No, no. [*Mastering himself.*] I spoke in good faith, Wadey. I spoke in good faith . . . and I am not afraid. [*Going towards him pitifully.*] Take me to her, Wadey; take me to her. . . . I will be with her at the end.

WADEBRIDGE. At the end she was alone. She is dead.

Conal O'Riordan, *Rope Enough* (Dublin, 1914).

CONAL HOLMES O'CONNELL O'RIORDAN was born in Dublin in 1874. He became a director of the Abbey in 1909 and revived *The Playboy* in spite of great opposition. His earlier work appeared under the pseudonym Norreys Connell. His first play *The Piper* was put on in the Abbey to a hostile reception. Later plays were *Rope Enough* (1913) *His Majesty's Pleasure* (1925) and *The King's Wooing* (1929). Though a career as a soldier was frustrated by a spine injury he managed to serve in both World Wars, as YMCA welfare officer and Air Raid Warden. Many of his novels are about the Service. He died in 1948.

The Zoological Gardens in Phoenix Park was founded in the early 1830's only a few years after the Jardin des Plantes in Paris and Regent's Park Zoo in London. It remains famous for its successful breeding of lions, records of which go back to 1857. The Royal Zoological Society of Ireland is its governing body, the President and Council meeting for breakfast every Saturday morning. This civilised practice has been going on for more than a hundred years.

*In the Zoo 1904* (Lawrence Collection, National Library).

To the intelligentsia of Dublin, this play might not appear a very striking drama. "Melodramatic propaganda" would probably be their description of it, but here in Ballycullen it was as one of the great Greek tragedies of old in Athens. For all his soul might have dwindled sadly in very truth, what man was there amongst them at all who had not spoken out of his dream sometime of dying for Ireland? Of how, maybe, as he went down some grass-grown boreen, where the hawthorn blossoms in Maytime fell and were blown on a light wind like fragrant, tinted snow, and for all its rich colour of the fields at sunset, the shadow over all had seemed to him the deadly shadow of England. And then he had spoken to the girl walking by his side, of "fighting the bloody British Government," of "Dying from a bullet in some rebellion or another," of being "murdered mebbe in jail, the way they murdered Wolfe Tone." "And waht whoud you do then?" Then there had come, probably, a little strained, beseeching look into the eyes of the girl as she put her soft arm about his neck, her brown, troubled head upon his shoulder, and sobbed her request that he would not go. And he had not gone, only marrying the girl a little later, and wondering ever since at the "wildness" of himself, and he a young fellow. No Irish dramatist had seen this material, and yet it was the complete expression in tragi-comedy of Ireland - the Ireland of all the dreams, and all the songs, and all the dying. Many a young man would be behaving just like this after to-night's performance, and both the young women and the old would be weeping little, silent tears as they tried to remember or to picture themselves in the disquieting, in fact desperate, position of Sara Curran. But over all the audience, over its face as one man, would be clouding a curious mixture of expression, combative, satirical, critical, comical, tragical really in its full significance.

Already Michael Dempsey had taken the Ballycullen Dramatic Class on to the stage, and they were all stiffly awaiting the rise of the curtain. One of the girls, she who was to play the part of Ann Devlin, complained of a little faintness, and someone rushed to get her a mineral. The man who was to play Michael Dwyer brought out a bottle of whiskey from his

pocket, and took a good, long drink. Then the littl drop-curtain which had been so badly painted b Ambrose Donohoe, the handy man, screeche upward, and the play began.

One might have seen immediately that although possessing the curious, intimate connectio with Irish life already suggested, it was made distan from Irish life by several focuses of unreality. I possessed no verisimilitude as a picture of the period and, in the second place, was no transcript of life inasmuch as the method of presentation was as fa removed from realism as it is possible for anything t be. And yet it did not appear as any kind o spontaneous romance; one could not call it folk-play. The lines were spoken haltingly, with poor accent, which did not fully express thei meaning. The entrances and exits and the situation were most crudely effected. Yet were the peopl gripped, for no other reason than because it was a pla about Robert Emmet. Indeed, Michael Dempse need not have gone to such pains to give a grea performance. Merely to have stood there on the ver middle of the stage in his top boots with gold tassels white trousers and black cut-away coat, his arm folded, and a lock of hair brushed down upon hi forehead, would have been quite sufficient. In fact from one aspect of Ballycullen's point of view, th whole thing was quite unnecessary. The drunke ballad-singers had told them all they wanted to know about Robert Emmet, and this was exactly how the had always seen Robert Emmet dressed up in picture. Into their dull minds was crowded a sudde warfare of conflicting thoughts.

Brinsley MacNamara, *The Clanking of Chain* (Dublin, 1920).

RINSLEY MACNAMARA was born John Weldon in the village of Delvin, Co Westmeath in 1890. He was actor, playwright, essayist and novelist, famous for two widely differing Irish 'classics', the novel *The Valley of the Squinting Windows* (1918) and the play, *Look at the Heffernans* (1926). The first caused a minor riot in his home village on the night of 28 May 1918 when a copy was publicly burnt. The second is a typical Abbey comedy still performed by many amateur companies throughout Ireland. The great achievement of MacNamara as stated fifty years ago by A E Malone was 'in assisting Ireland to see itself as something less than a nation of demi-gods'. Two novels, *The Clanking of Chains* (1920) and *The Mirror in the Dusk* (1928) in different ways contribute to the removal of this romantic myopia, the first in its account of the disillusionment of the Nationalist dream and the second in its truth about Irish rural life. He died in 1963.

*Cast of play in Father Mathew Hall, 1917* (Old Athlone Society).

*Skating at Johnstown Castle, Co Wexford c. 1885*
(Séamas de Vál Collection, Oulart).

BRIGHT sunshine, pure invigorating air, and ice in perfect condition had combined to make Miss Fetherstone's skating party an emphatic success. The young people from the Rectory were there, and a few more - considering the depleted condition of the neighbourhood, it was quite a considerable gathering; but no one ever refused an invitation to the Priory, however short the notice. All day the picturesque banks of the pond had echoed merry laughter and ceaseless chaff, and the ice-imprisoned Undine in the depths had hummed a welcome to the steel-shod feet which had never ceased to plough its frozen surface. Even now, when the afternoon was fast giving place to night, and stars began to twinkle here and there in the darkening blue above, enthusiastic skaters were still pursuing each other in games, or taking station for quadrilles on the smooth, grey ice.

Kate and Gerald were slowly climbing the steep path that led up to the house. She looked very handsome, a tall graceful figure in her furs, and recent exercise had given to her cheeks the touch of colour which they sometimes lacked.

Gerald walked beside her, swinging a pair of skates in either hand. Earlier in the day he had found opportunity to acquaint her with the recent occurrences at Liscarrick, but their conversation had been interrupted and fragmentary, as occasion served. Now he had given her the whole tale, beginning with the Squireen's proposal to Mrs. Delaney, and going on to Molly's adventure on the Bog road, and her understanding, as yet unannounced, with Jack Whalen.

Miss Fetherstone was deeply concerned. She was genuinely delighted at the news of Molly's engagement to her cousin, and was already considering in her warm heart what she could do to make smoother their path for the young lovers, but Mrs. Delaney's position and the attitude she assumed moved her at once to pity and anger.

"It's incredible!" she cried hotly. "That a woman in your sister-in-law's position could stoop to even *think* of such a creature as O'Hara. Why, the man drinks, if there were nothing else."

"I don't think Emmie knows that," said Gerald.

"But she's bound to find it out, sooner or later."

"Yes," he assented, "she's bound to find it out, and if I can manage it, it will be sooner, not later."

George H Jessop, *The Shamrock Grows* (1911).

GEORGE H JESSOP was born in Dublin in 1850 and went to America after graduating from TCD. He was editor of *Judge* and contributed to other humorous papers. His collection of sketches, *Gerald French's Friend* (1889) deals with the adventures of a prodigal Irishman in the US and of the characteristic immigrant Irish types he meets on his travels. The piece printed from *The Shamrock Grows* (1911) is about the Ireland of the latter-day squireens when the horse still had a higher place in society than most humans and all endings were happy. He died in 1915 in Hampstead having become a Catholic shortly before his death.

At last the waltz died languorously away, and he led her into the hall. "Shall we go out to the terrace, or would it be too cold outside?" he asked, with an unconscious note of pleading in his voice.

"No, it's not cold now; besides, I have a wrap here," Zoe answered, picking up a light cloak from one of the hall chairs, and throwing it round her shoulders.

"Good," said Barry, and they went out.

Miss Delaney's house was delightfully situated - high up on Killiney Hill, among tall trees, and commanding a full view of the bay from Bray Head on the south side right round to the Hill of Howth on the north-east. When the two reached the terrace, they stood for a moment lookng out over the sea, enjoying the fresh night air after the heat inside. A yellow moon was shining, and the low murmur of the sea came to them, borne on the faint breeze that gently stirred the trees. The night was beautifully fine, and quite warm now, and yet there was a vague, elusive something of sadness in the air, the regretful brooding of autumn.

"What a night!" Barry murmured, by way of marking time, for he was rather in a whirl.

"Delicious - beautiful!" Zoe answered, and she really meant it and felt it - but still she was fingering her trinkets and patting her hair.

"Let us go round to the side - it's quieter there - will you?" said Barry after a moment, again with the unconscious pleading note. He had the rare gift of a deep musical voice, and sincere emotion gives to that sort of voice most compelling inflections. Zoe felt its charm and its appeal; she gave him a little quick nod of the head and a smile. "If you like," she agreed. He led her round to the south side of the house, and then along to the end of that part of the terrace.

"We don't want to sit down, do we?" she said, going to the edge and leaning on the low stone balustrade.

"Whatever you like," said Barry, coming near to her. "I'd sooner have this - as the only seat is in the shadow there."

Then there fell a silence as they stood in the moonlight, the man, as he watched her hungrily, too oppressed with feeling to be able to find a word, and the girl, staring at the distant misty hills of Wicklow, seemingly quite unconscious of her companion's eager glances, but only seemingly.

W F Casey, *Zoë* (London, 1911)

W F CASEY is chiefly famous for two plays *The Man Who Missed the Tide* and *The Suburban Groove* which were presented in the Abbey in 1908. These dealt, unusually for the time and place with upper middle class characters in Dublin. *Zoë* (1911) deals with the same social class and is an account of the heartless flirtations of the eponymous heroine in a city mainly dedicated to golf, bridge and theatre. Casey afterwards became editor of the London *Times*.

*Couple outside the Royal Irish Yacht Club Kingstown
c. 1901* (Lawrence Collection, National Library).

## IRISH ASTRONOMY
*A Veritable Myth, Touching the Constellation of O'Ryan,*
*Ignorantly and Falsely Spelled Orion.*

O'Ryan was a man of might
  Whin Ireland was a nation,
But poachin' was his heart's delight
  And constant occupation.
He had an ould militia gun,
  And sartin sure his aim was;
He gave the keepers many a run,
  And wouldn't mind the game laws.

St. Pathrick wanst was passin' by
  O'Ryan's little houldin',
And, as the saint felt wake and dhry,
  He thought he'd enther bould in.
"O'Ryan," says the saint, "avick!
  To praich at Thurles I'm goin',
So let me have a rasher quick,
  And a dhrop of Innishowen."

"No rasher will I cook for you
  While betther is to spare, sir,
But here's a jug of mountain dew,
  And there's a rattlin' hare, sir."
St. Pathrick he looked mighty sweet,
  And says he, "Good luck attind you,
And, when you're in your winding-sheet,
  It's up to heaven I'll sind you."

O'Ryan gave his pipe a whiff -
  "Them tidin's is transportin',
But may I ax your saintship if
  There's any kind of sportin'?"
St. Pathrick said, "A Lion's there,
  Two Bears, a Bull, and Cancer" -
"Bedad," says Mick, "the huntin's rare;
  St. Pathrick, I'm your man, sir."

So, to conclude my song aright,
  For fear I'd tire your patience,
You'll see O'Ryan any night
  Amid the constellations.
And Venus follows in his track
  Till Mars grows jealous raally.
But faith, he fears the Irish knack
  Of handling the shillaly.

Charles Graham Halpine, 'Irish Astronomy' in *Irish Literature IV*
(Philadelphia, 1904).

CHARLES GRAHAM HALPINE alias 'Pte Myles O'Reilly' was born in Oldcastle, Co Meath in 1829, the son of the rector, the Rev N J Halpin (the 'e' he added later). A student at TCD he did not graduate but followed a career in journalism which took him to America. At the outbreak of Lincoln's war he joined the famous 'FIghting 69th' and rose to the rank of general. He enrolled the first negro regiment in the Federal Army and was placed high on the Southern States' blacklist. His songs, including 'Not a star from the flag shall fade' were very popular throughout the army and the north United States. He died in 1868 after an accidental overdose of chloral, taken to cure insomnia.

The 'Leviathan of Parsonstown' as it was christened remained the largest telescope in the world until 1917. Its six-foot diameter enabled the local clergyman to walk right through it, a distance of fifty-eight feet when it was opened in 1845. The builder of the telescope, the third earl of Rosse, discovered that the *nebulae* was a star system separate from our galaxy and many millions of miles further away than had been thought.

*Telescope at Birr Castle 1889* (Lawrence Collection, National Library).

"Rock candy is sweet, but it isn't soft!" flashed Sadie.

"Yes," retorted Katie, " and you're soft, but you aren't sweet!"

"You must say what's in the script!"

"I'm only an amateur!" cried Katie shrilly; "I won't be 'musted'!"

"It's plain to be seen that you are only an amateur," was the crushing retort.

"And I," Shaun announced, wearily passing his fingers through his dark hair, "happen to be stage manager. Go on with the play."

"Why doesn't my husband write to me?" lamented Mrs. O'Grady, her voice rising and falling like the *keen* of a Banshee.

"Good heavens!" exclaimed Brian, quite astounded; "is that a new bit in the play?"

"Of course it isn't," snapped his sister; "Hold your tongue, Belinda, and prompt!"

"My name is Brigid," wailed the prompter, "and if I hold my tongue, how can I prompt?"

"Proceed, 'Viola,'" said Shaun, in dull tones.

"'How softly the sun sinks to rest! The -'"

"But you know," interrupted Denis, "that's a foolish expression! How else could the sun sink?"

"I know of a place where it sets with an unearthly bang." Patsy informed them.

"Where's that?" was the breathless inquiry.

"Kingstown, Dublin."

"After these two exhibitions of crass ignorance," remarked Shaun dryly, "we will proceed with the play."

Katie began again, accordingly: "'How softly the sun sinks to rest! The golden glory in the west -'" here she stopped, and appealed to Shaun.

"Is it supposed to be poetry?" she asked.

"*No!*"

"'Shines,'" continued Katie, "'like - like -'"

"You're all wrong, " interposed Mrs. O'Grady; "begin all over again."

"Why didn't you prompt?"

"You wouldn't take the last prompt!"

Katie's retort was interrupted by the entrance of Barney, cheery, debonair, and inclined to be a little dictatorial.

"Sorry to be so late," said he, "but I met Thady O'Reilly, and he kept me. I mean, I kept him."

"What's he doing?" asked Brian, "getting drunk, I suppose!"

"Certainly not," returned Barney, "Thady is always sober as a judge, and as foolish too."

"I was rehearsing the first scene, Mr. O'Hagan," Katie told him, with great dignity.

"Then go ahead," said Barney, beginning, as usual, to stage-manage the whole thing.

"'How softly'" began Katie, for the third time, "'the sun sinks to -'"

"Oh, speak up, Viola!" advised Barney; "why you wouldn't be heard without ear trumpets!"

"People don't usually shout their sentimental sentiments."

"Neither do they mumble them."

Mary B Pearse, *The Murphys of Ballystack* (Dublin, 1917).

MARY BRIDGET (afterwards Brigid) PEARSE was born in Dublin in 1893, the youngest sister of Padraig. She was an eager recipient of his youthful romanticism, deprecated his later militarism and was estranged from the family after 1916. She compiled a family history in 1919 but this led to further dispute with her sister Margaret. She wrote, acted in and produced many plays but her main publication was a sub-Somerville and Ross account of small town Irish life, *The Murphys of Ballystack* (1917). It was the country viewed from the town in a sentimentalised and condescending way and the writing notably lacks the Irish cousin's experience, talent and bite. She died in 1947 after a history of recurring neurosis.

*The Corsican Brothers* (1856) was one of the most famous of the romantic melodramas specially devised for the aristocratic theatregoers of mid-century London and New York. The London impresario most closely associated with the play was Charles Kean, the son of the great Irish Regency actor, Edmund Kean. This story of twin brothers who feel each other's pain became vastly popular. In the major London theatres of the time stage machinery had reached its peak of ingenuity and a remarkable device made specially for the play and known since as the Corsican trap allowed a ghost to seem to rise and drift across the stage. Boucicault brought the play to Ireland and its popularity with amateur groups became as great as that of Boucicault's own successes, *The Colleen Bawn* and *The Shaughraun*.

Cast of *The Corsican Brothers*, Carlow Lay College 1886 (St Patrick's College, Carlow).

111

The station consists of a small shed built of stone, with a slated roof, somewhat out of repair, and containing a single wooden bench for the benefit of waiting passengers. The inner walls of this edifice are chipped and grimy, and their decoration is furnished by railway time-tables (generally a month or two out of date - a trifling drawback, since nobody ever dreams of consulting them), interspersed with large posters announcing weekly and monthly fairs, and auction bills regarding sales of hay and oats and other farm produce. In another small box-like erection at one end of the platform, and close beside the solitary gate which gives ingress and egress to the station, is the ticket-office. Within it the station-master sits with the utmost official pomp, and from it he directs the activities of his sole subordinate, a youth of some sixteen summers, who might, from his chief's manner, be a complete staff at a large terminus rather than one forlorn-looking lad. The arrival of a train brings forth the station-master to the platform with an air of great grandeur. There is quite a touch of magnificence in the manner in which, when "she is signalled from the Junction," he emerges from the ticket-office, locking the door behind him. Descending passengers are treated strictly according to their class. First-class (rare birds these) with high distinction, third-class with contumely, and second-class (to which most of us adhere) with moderate respect, pleasingly informed with cordiality according to the place we occupy in Mooney's affections,

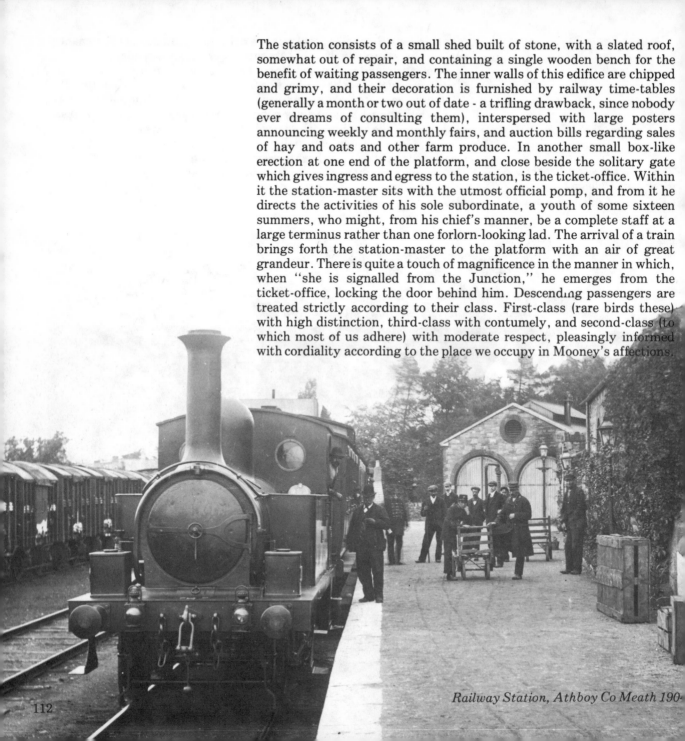

*Railway Station, Athboy Co Meath 190-*

112

For Bartholomey Mooney, station-master of Aghole, is a respecter of persons undisguisedly and deliberately, and his high esteem of the qualities fitted for his own office does not include impartiality. Indeed, a less impartial person it would be difficult to discover - even in Ireland. This is the more remarkable since, according to his own account, his favourite axiom is: "Be civil to all, but familiar with few." So far as his practice goes, the reverse would be more correct, for he is familiar with almost everybody and civil to none.

Ella MacMahon *Irish Vignettes* (London, 1928).

The station was exceedingly clean; and when we left it, and an erect, intelligent, well-dressed station-man, who at about half a mile from it, in a well appointed uniform, appeared standing on the green bank, motionless as a statue, I could not help feeling that his outstretched arm not only showed us the way we were to go, but, morally speaking, demonstrated most indisputably the facility with which a railway, wherever it runs, establishes habits of order, discipline and cleanliness, which would have been declared impossible to inculcate.

Sir Franci B Head *A Fortnight in Ireland* (London, 1952).

ELLA MAC MAHON was daughter of the Rev J H MacMahon who was chaplain to the Lord Lieutenant of Ireland in the '90's'. Her best of about twenty novels deals with working-class seduction and betrayal, the critical event, taking place on an Easter Monday excursion to Bray. The piece printed, a pen-picture of a station-master, is typical of her style and comes from *Irish Vignettes* (1928).

*Railway Station, Dundalk 1910* (Lawrence Collection, National Library).

# Index of Authors

Alexander, A.F. .............. 56
Alexander, M. .............. 87
Anderson, P. .............. 88
Armstrong, G.F. .............. 23
Boyle, W. (2) .............. 17
Byrne, F. .............. 72
Casey, W.F. .............. 106
Childers, R.E. .............. 46
Clarke, J.I.C. .............. 78
Colum, P. .............. 13
Craig, (Rev.) J.D. .............. 41
D'Arcy, H. .............. 32
Figgis, D. .............. 96
Gogarty, O.St.J. (2) .............. 76
Graves, A.P. .............. 60
Hall, (Mrs.) S.C. .............. 64
Halpine, C.G. .............. 108
Head, F.B. .............. 113
Hopper, N. .............. 53
Jessop, G.H. .............. 105
Joyce, J. .............. 25
Le Fanu, S. .............. 44
Letts, W. .............. 39
Locke, J. .............. 37
Lynam, (Col.) W.F. .............. 54
Lynch, H. .............. 74
McCall, P.J. .............. 63
McCarthy, D.F. .............. 94
MacMahon, E. .............. 112
MacNamara, B. .............. 102
Moylan, T.K. .............. 28
Murphy, J.L. .............. 40
Murphy, N.P. .............. 20
O'Brien, R.B. .............. 87
O'Casey, S. .............. 66, 92
O'Riordan, C. ('Norreys Connell') .101
Pearse, M.B. .............. 110
Pearse, P.H. .............. 98
Rathkyle, M.A. .............. 14
Rolleston, T.W. .............. 30
Sigerson. D. .............. 42

Stacpoole, H.de V. .............. 26
Stephens, J. (2) .............. 58
Stoker, B. .............. 81
Synge, J.M. .............. 10
Tynan, K. .............. 84

# Bibliography

F S L Lyons. *Ireland since the famine* (London, 1973)
Patrick Flanagan. *Transport in ireland.* (Dublin, 1969)
Lennox Robinson. *Ireland's Abbey Theatre* — a history 1899-1915 . (London, 1951)
S J Brown. *Ireland in Fiction.* (Dublin, 1919)
D J O'Donoghue. *The poets of Ireland.* (Dublin, 1912)
B T Cleeve. *Dictionary of Irish writers.* (Cork, 1967-1971)
M Brown. *The politics of Irish literature.* (London, 1971)
U O'Connor. *Oliver St John Gogarty.* (London, 1964)

# Acknowledgements

For kind permission to reprint copyright material the followin▮ acknowledgements are made: to James Duffy & Co Ltd for T ▮ Moylan; to Mr O Weldon for Brinsley MacNamara; to Dolmen Pres▮ Ltd for Padraic Colum; to Gill & Macmillan Ltd for M B Pearse; t▮ Macmillan and Co Ltd for Sean O'Casey and James Stephens; and t▮ Jonathan Cape for James Joyce.

For kind permission to use photographs acknowledgements ar▮ made to the National Library of Ireland; Larry O'Connor, M▮ Matthews of Killeigh, Co Offaly; Michael Byrne, Offaly Researc▮ Library; Séamas de Vál S P; Gárda Síochána Museum; Old Kilkenn▮ Society; Arnold Crawford: Library of T C D. Every effort has bee▮ made to trace the owners of copyright material used in this book. In th▮ event of omission, the publisher would be glad of notification.

*King Edward at Maynooth*

(Lawrence Collection, National Library).

*Fitzwilliam Square, Wicklow* (Lawrence Collection, National Library).

*North Earl Street, Dublin*